JOURNEY

Paco Rabanne is one of the world's most renowned couturiers. He made his name as the designer of metallic dresses and also went on to produce a series of original perfumes, the latest of which, Paco for men, is a bestselling favourite.

JOURNEY

From One Life to Another

Paco Rabanne

ELEMENT

Shaftesbury, Dorset ● Rockport, Massachusetts
Brisbane, Queensland

© Element Books Limited 1997
Text © Éditions Michael Lafon 1991

First published in Great Britain in 1997 by
Element Books Limited
Shaftesbury, Dorset SP7 8BP

Published in the USA in 1997 by
Element Books, Inc.
PO Box 830, Rockport, MA 01966

Published in Australia in 1997 by
Element Books Limited
for Jacaranda Wiley Limited
33 Park Road, Milton, Brisbane 4064

Translation by Marcia de Brito
Cover design by Bridgewater Book Company
Text illustrations by Paco Rabanne
Designed and typeset by Linda Reed and Joss Nizan
Printed and bound in Great Britain by Creative Print & Design
Group, (Wales) Ebbw Vale

British Library Cataloguing in Publication
Data available

Library of Congress Cataloging in Publication
Data available

ISBN 1–86204–005–2

Contents

Acknowledgement

A designer never achieves a dress or a coat completely by himself. He creates the line and the movement, draws the sketch and chooses the material, after which a team puts his ideas into practice. As far as this book is concerned, my thanks go to the Huguette Maure–Olivier de Broca team!

Preface

❧❦❧

At the time of his first collection, in January 1964, Paco diverted metal from its usual functions to dress the 'amazons of feminine emancipation' in a style which looked very close to the chain-mail of knights of old. On the podium, amid the usual white, often blond models, favourites for the job until then, stood magnificent black models moving to the music. This was unheard of, incredible! Half the audience left, scandalized, while the rest enthusiastically welcomed the entrance of contemporary art into the world of traditional couture.

Indifferent to the confusion, Paco Rabanne returned to his workshop to forge the fashion of the future, and Calandre, his symbolic perfume, sprinkled its balm over every continent. Soon no fashion show took place without steely ornaments or exotic beauties. Today, numerous young designers are also working with aluminium laminae, patches of Rhodoid and reflecting steel, all following the inspiration of this 1960s revolutionary who even then knew that he was preparing for the future millennium.

During the spring of 1990, 26 years after his debut, Paco Rabanne received the Gold Thimble in professional recognition of a style which had become classic and showed no signs of losing its appeal. If such a man speaks to us of his vision of God and confesses to us that he wanders through previous lives as others do through their childhood memories and that he has relationships with spirits, it cannot be believed for a moment, that he should be doing so to attract attention. This mystic has no reason to play at mystifying others; he does not need this kind of trick to attain fortune and success.

Mademoiselle Chanel called him a 'metallurgist', but this is not someone playing at being Vulcan: you need only see him at a presentation, leaving backstage, harassed, quickly bowing in response to the honours and then looking desperately for an opening in the curtain through which to disappear. Nor is he, as some people have thought, a man who wants to found a sect, or be a prophet, or exercise power over others. Paco is in fact a believer and an adept in solitary meditation. In truth, this book rather scared him. The TV interviews during which he was questioned on his various reincarnations earned him millions of enthusiastic letters, as well as some too ardent and some irritatingly sarcastic. A public basically thirsty for anecdotes is not always interested in a spiritual search.

Paco Rabanne is not offering comfortable spiritual cures for anguish. His own path, since the age of seven, has been beset with traps and false interpretations, but along with it have come many revelations. People close to Paco Rabanne, and his spiritual guides, have urged him to overcome his reticence and share his testimony of this spiritual journey. This book, which started with interviews which I conducted, was an exhilarating experience from which I have not yet recovered. The book retraces the picaresque adventure of Paco's past existences. It refers to alchemy, oriental religions, the first Christians and passages in the Gospel. The author, from the first few pages, embarks on a daring description of his astral voyages, the first of which dates back to childhood. Whether we have been, many centuries ago, Grand Inquisitor or washerwoman, Paco Rabanne reminds us that we are reincarnated to lighten our karma and to access higher spiritual planes. It is here and now that we must deal with this, without despising our present body or ignoring our social obligations. He even gives some advice on how to master time, increase our capacity for concentration, refine our intuitive faculties and administer success, without falling into the trap of relying on New Age panaceas and keeping in mind that what is important is beyond these earthly interests.

The main interest for the author lies in the quest for the knowledge which leads to 'divine light' and there this initiate, who still holds on to his artisan's overall, gives proof of his wisdom. He warns us against undue fascination with esotericism, against supernatural gifts exploited without prudence, and he reminds us of the legendary mishaps of sorcerers' apprentices. He invites us to open our eyes to the symbolism contained in all things (fashion provides fascinating examples) and to blossom through meditation and cosmic love. And it should be done quickly! For according to this designer we are living near the end of linear time. The apocalypse approaches, that is to say not the end of the world, but the end of this world – a time of revelation and the 'saving of the just'. There is more than one coincidence between the prophecies contained in the sacred texts and contemporary events and it should be enough to trouble and disturb us.

Paco Rabanne refuses to speak about the money he gives and his support for unknown artists and ethnic minorities, but I have seen some of the numerous letters he receives after his conferences. In these letters members of the audience thank him for having shown them the way to an acceptance of temporary injustice and suffering and even for helping them deal with the terror of death. He has rekindled in them courage and the long term hope which comes from submitting to an apprenticeship in humility: all conveyed with a touch of humour typical of the man.

I hope the readers of this book will reap similar benefits, and that they will find that Paco Rabanne showed them the way too.

Huguette Maure

1

The Silver Thread

Real life is elsewhere.
ARTHUR RIMBAUD

When my mother tiptoed into the bedroom I shared with my brother and leant over my bed, she was surprised to find me awake, wide-eyed and staring at the ceiling, incapable of finding rest in this world I had been thrown into by birth.

My mother reassured herself by thinking that I was probably a light sleeper and that I woke when she approached. But I knew very well that this was not so and that I sometimes spent whole nights waiting for the moment when finally I would succumb to fatigue. This insomnia was soon to become a veritable torture for me, rendered even more unbearable by the deep sleep in which my brother was immersed in the bed next to mine. I used to turn towards him sometimes and observe, without understanding, why nature had made us so different from one another.

To fight these long, empty and boring hours, as soon as I had learned to read, I devoured all the books I could lay my hands on. Unfortunately, this treatment had no great effect. Time continued to linger obstinately. Bedtime soon began to haunt me. Whereas my brother slept a leaden sleep, I followed the incessant rounds of my thoughts and listened to the chiming of the hours by the village bell. Occasionally numbed, my lucidity nevertheless refused to surrender and sink into unconsciousness, an affliction which greatly disturbed me.

One day, at the age of seven, no longer able to bear my lack of sleep I decided, literally, to 'kill time', that is to say not to elude it, as I had done with reading, but to stop it. To do so, I instinctively applied a technique which consisted of listening to my heartbeats and submitting my breathing to their rhythm, creating a total void in my spirit. Completely absorbed in the quest for that harmony between my pulse and my breathing, I closed my eyes and pressed my eyelids, putting pressure on the iris according to that same cardiac rhythm. At that moment an extraordinary thing happened. As I was lying on my bed, conscious, time stood still. A lead sheet fell on my body. I was incapable of moving even a finger, flattened by these tons of matter which oppressed and nailed me to the mattress.

A growing disquiet took hold of me, but I did not even have time to dwell on it. Suddenly, I was projected at an incredible speed into an immense tunnel with silvery walls. It was as if I was riding a roller-coaster. All of a sudden I emerged from this tunnel and found myself very high in an intensely dark blue sky, in a firmament where stars of an extraordinary luminosity shone. What ineffable pleasure it was to float in total silence in that universe of peace and light as opposed to the noisy and furious world in which I lived at the time. Looking down I saw myself, or rather I saw my body lying beside that of my brother, sleeping in a tiny room. I was held by a silver thread which undulated in space, floating and meandering; and which joined my floating self, that ethereal 'me', to my physical body which rested so far away. The 'thread of the Virgin' carried me on an astral voyage, an umbilical cord connecting me to the telluric matrix.

In spite of the astonishing beauty of the cosmos in which I floated, I suddenly panicked: I imagined that, as I was no longer in my material envelope, anybody down there could take hold and slip into it in my place. I also feared that by venturing too far I would break this string which linked me to my body and to earth. What would happen if this silver thread broke?

But how could I re-enter? I then mentally asked my body to move its right hand: I gave it an order to stir, even if only the index finger. At the precise instant this happened I was sucked downwards, but this return, this transmutation, was extraordinarily painful. In effect, my energetic body was much more extended than my physical one and I had enormous trouble reintegrating into it, for to do so I needed to condense and compress myself into matter. With enormous effort and considerable pain, I finally regained my bedroom's four walls with my heart racing, exhausted but somewhat exhilarated.

This prodigious adventure, which I could not yet quite understand, was to disturb my whole life. From that day on, I felt transformed. It was as if that experience had awakened me to another world, to somewhere beyond, on the other side, a place which I knew nothing about but which I intuitively felt existed. I recalled the puppet shows I had seen in the village square: on the black velvet of the stage, one could perceive the strings which indicated the presence of a superior will that gave life to the wax and rag dolls. My silver thread held me to earthly life but seemed to point, simultaneously, the way to heaven, to the cosmos: Ariadne's thread which would guide me in my personal path.

Since then, without at first being completely conscious of it, I committed myself to taking the long path to truth. I became an initiate, not the owner of any secret, but an apprentice of knowledge, the traveller whose only baggage is an insatiable curiosity.

I was born in 1934 in the Spanish part of the Basque country, in the province of Guipúzcoa, near San Sebastián, in a village called Passages de San Pedro, St Peter's Passages. My real name is Francisco Rabaneda Cuervo, Francis Slice-of-Bread Crow.

I can safely say that my childhood was in no way 'normal'. In fact, my first years were spent in a very precarious environment, side by side with death and suffering, on the roads of a long exodus, at the mercy of the hazardous events of a civil war, which was followed by a world war: that was the only daily reality I knew.

That violent universe seemed to be my family's fate. My maternal grandfather was one of the first Spanish socialists killed by the Civil Guard. My father, initially a colonel in the king's army, joined the side of the Republicans after the exile of King Alfonso XIII in 1934, following the elections which installed the Republic. Two years later, the Popular Front was victorious. Exiled to the Canary Islands, General Franco provoked an uprising in Morocco which, instigated by the royalists and the Catholic hierarchy, triggered a civil war under the pretext of restoring the monarchy. With the help of Italian and German contingents, he took power and held onto it for the next 45 years.

My father led the Republican forces of the northern region. His position of leadership obliged him to be continually on the front line, always moving and we had to follow him everywhere. These are my first memories: picking up clothes in a hurry, walking through the countryside, climbing up on a horse-cart or sometimes on the back of a rickety truck, always between two improvised camps, exposed to the bombs and machine-guns, with the result that I quickly learned to estimate their danger. The Spanish Civil War was extremely bloody – 1 million dead. As a very young child I witnessed terrible scenes and death quickly became a part of my universe.

Always in my father's tow, the Rabaneda family found itself in Guernica, in the Basque country, when the town was bombed by German planes in May 1937. I was then only three years old, but I hold a vivid memory of that inferno. My mother made me put pencils in my mouth before falling asleep, so as not to be a victim of the exploding bombs which fell nearby. People succumbed, for they did not know that one must keep the mouth open to avoid exploding due to the compression of the thoracic cage.

This bombing of a civil population by the sinister 'Condor' legion caused worldwide indignation. Picasso dedicated his famous painting *Guernica* to this tragedy, with its bitter black and white tones, its trampled dismembered bodies and faces turned upwards towards an unjust heaven. Guernica was sacrificed: Guernica, that holy town of the Basques where stands the legendary sacred tree of knowledge, symbol of Atlantis, that lost paradise from whence the Basques say they came. The Basque country, was immersed in chaos as that mysterious continent had been in the past.

In 1939 we were forced to leave Spain. Franco's armies had managed to cut the Republican territory in two and were busy exterminating the pockets of resistance. Barcelona, last bastion of Republicanism, fell in January 1939. My father was captured and executed. My mother, frantic with pain, took us, my grandmother, my sisters, my brother and myself, on a journey to cross the Pyrenean mountain paths to reach France, the only escape route from a mortal trap. On foot, through the snow and cold and at the mercy of air raids, we managed to cross the border.

After a time in the internment camps of Port-Vendres and Collioure, we took refuge in Brittany. In Morlaix we were housed by a French socialist, a deputy for the Finistère region. But we still had not found a haven of peace, far from it. Some months later, the German Panzerdivisionen invaded the north of France and I remember my fright at seeing the SS arrive in their black shirts, with their dogs in tow. The Gestapo was looking for Spanish refugees to send them back to Spain, where they would be executed by Franco. Soon the French embarked on the so-called 'rail battle', meaning the sabotage of means of transport and communication; in retaliation the SS carried out raids and shot the hostages. We lived in a semi-clandestine state, constantly on our guard. In Brittany, as in the rest of occupied France, there reigned an atmosphere of permanent terror.

Having been brought up with no pampering, I had an astonishing maturity for my age, like all children of war. At five years of age, I was already an adult. Forced by circumstances, I learned very early on to keep my senses on alert and observe what went on around me. I soon became conscious that there were two realities. In Spain, I had lived in a country divided between Francoists and Republicans. In occupied France, there were the 'maquisards', as the members of the resistance were called, and the collaborators. In Brittany, at one point, we lived opposite the Kommandantur. There, while still a young child, I remember seeing, when night fell, French people skittering close to the walls, their collars up, coming to denounce their neighbours. The world had two faces: there was always a daytime face and a hidden one.

But I found the best illustration of the world's duality in the opposition between my mother and my grandmother. My mother, who was first seamstress in Balenciaga's couture house, and then an important member of the Spanish socialist party, was a staunch materialist, a resolute atheist. Traditionally my family stood politically very much to the left. Fiercely anti-clerical, she saw in religion nothing but 'opium for the people'.

But I had a grandmother who, being the black sheep of the family, was deeply religious. Every morning she would rise at dawn to go to mass. Her faith would gladly encompass white magic, which is to say occultism. She had inherited from her grandmother the secrets of nature and knew how to heal with plants. Of all her grandchildren I was, without doubt, her favourite. I spent a lot of time with her, she would tell me the 'secrets of the broom' and of kitchen salt. From her I learned many things: how to recognize a plant, its uses, the hours when our organs are receptive to its influence, the different power of the roots, the stem and the flower.

I was, therefore, divided between these two forms of knowledge: my mother's which was Cartesian and materialist and my grandmother's magic knowledge or rather witch-like wisdom. But the two did not strike me as contradictory: they constituted two facets of the same reality which had to be constantly interpreted, no matter what the values expressed by these very different reference systems.

The Rabaneda-Cuervo family preserved a genealogical tree, ordered by my grandfather, which went back to the year 600 – a date which marked the arrival of a certain Celtic clan on the Santander mountain. Their emblem, the crow, was sculpted on the keystone of the vaulted entrance to the family farm. The *cuervo*, these crows, as legend has it, guided the Francs who journeyed from the Ural Mountains to France. The crow, sacred bird of the Asian gods, was sent to earth on the eve of wars; their crowing foretold the number of dead. The crow, Merlin's fetish bird, was holder of the key which opened the hidden place where nature kept its secrets. The crow was the first bird to leave Noah's ark, even before the dove, to verify if the earth had again emerged from the waters.

When, at the age of seven, I experienced my first astral voyage, it was in my grandmother that I confided as a matter of course. This was all the more necessary because after several experiences of this type, I started feeling intense burns, as if daggers were being thrust into me, in several precise points of my body. During the day, on the way to school, I was

7

suddenly assailed by strong pains in my heart, my throat and my belly. My grandmother treated these ailments by giving me a small glass of Aniseed del Mono to drink, an aniseed beverage with 45° of alcohol. 'Drink, it will calm you.' And so it did. Without knowing the origin of these pains, I could not help but associate them with my ethereal body's 'comings and goings'. Later, thanks to the practice of yoga, I learned that the human body possesses a certain number of energetic centres called '*chakras*'. Through these junction points the '*kundalîni*', the vital force, circulates, like a kind of serpent entwined around the spinal column. The Hindus consider that the opening of these chakras is the starting point for entering into harmony with the world. My out-of-body excursions had awoken the kundalîni and consequently there was an inner transmutation which took me little by little to a higher level. Obviously I had no knowledge, at that time, about kundalîni or the chakras, even less of the secrets of Hindu wisdom, but it was not long before I experienced signs of the awakening of that inner force.

During my silent moments, I gradually began to see precise images forming before my eyes. At first they were static maps, snapshots of senseless worlds, of extraordinary landscapes, unknown places, clips from ages gone by, of royal courts and austere temples consecrated to some unfamiliar cult. Slowly these images became animated. The snapshots became film sequences and I soon noticed that they evolved around a central protagonist, who appeared under different guises. Suddenly, I became conscious that this personage was none other than myself, in multiple corporeal envelopes! One can imagine what confusion such intuition can create in a seven-year-old child, or in any adult for that matter! Where did these visions come from? From which buried memories had they sprung?

At first, I tried to tell my mother about them and she replied in her usual Cartesian manner:

'Oh, it's your imagination again, playing tricks on you!'

She attributed that fertile imagination to the innumerable books I had read as a child to fight against my insomnia. But what I read then was in the field of children's literature, belonging to the 'Pink Library', featuring authors such as the Countess of Ségur or Jules Verne, which in no way corresponded to the images of violence, the scenes of Baroque sumptuousness and the strange universes which were, nevertheless, strangely familiar, which I perceived during my waking dreams. I had no references which would allow me to recreate such scenarios in my imagination. I would discover these later, when I was studying architecture at the Académie des Beaux Arts, suddenly recognizing in Egyptian iconography or Japanese engravings, the setting of some of my visions.

How could I have, at the age of seven, in a hamlet in Brittany in 1941, faithfully visualized places situated thousands of miles away? And one must remember the conditions of life at that time! Today a child has access, via 'the little screen', to the whole world. He knows, as if he had actually seen them, American skyscrapers, Inca pyramids or the Great Wall of China. But in that small locality in Brittany named Ploujean, in the middle of the war, we were cut off from everything. When a peddler passed through, people stopped and asked: 'Who are you? Where do you come from? What can you tell us?' And in the largest house of the hamlet a fire would be made, potatoes were baked on the coals and the peddler would sit down, proud of his importance. We would spend the night there, listening to stories about his life, his work, his troubles, his meetings and the rumours which prevailed in the main town. That was how information circulated. Those images – those flashes as we would call them today – therefore seemed supernatural to me, for they did not correspond to anything that I might have seen or heard.

But I did not insist. I gave up trying to convince my mother. An inner voice warned: 'Be quiet! Danger! Be quiet!' Faced with maternal incomprehension, I preferred to keep these visions to myself. They became my secret garden. I therefore kept silent. But slowly the idea that I had been 'another' yet the 'same', in a distant past, began to dawn on me and I realized that it was snippets of these previous lives that had surfaced in my memory.

One day I had a terrible vision, a veritable shock which left me in an indescribable state of agitation. Lying on my bed I found myself in that waking-dream state in which the erring spirit slowly detaches itself from the body before being sucked into sleep's black hole. All of a sudden I was enveloped by a blinding light into which my soul seemed to become diluted. I was transported into another world . . . and another time. I had, in fact, the certainty of reliving a scene which belonged to the recent past.

A voice told me: 'You are approaching the seventh energy level.'

Faced with a vibrating source of light, I was invaded by a sublime joy. Then twenty-four old men appeared: they were in fact huge luminous 'X's which I called old men, although they did not possess human form, for they seemed to me to be as ancient as the world.

'The time has come for you to return to earth', they said to me.

But I heard myself protest: 'No, I have done my time. I do not want to return.'

'Look!' they said.

Unfortunately I turned my head. I saw the blue planet. I saw, paraded before my eyes, everything that was going to happen on earth, from my birth to my death. It was a terrible spectacle of barbaric genocides, the convulsions of a disoriented humanity and apocalyptic plagues. Even as I confide these visions, the world has already suffered some of these atrocities, but the worst is yet to come.

The old men revealed to me what my destiny would be on earth. To assume it I would have to put on an envelope of flesh.

'Choose!' they said.

I then saw several couples making love on earth, surrounded by a phosphorescent halo. Each offered me a different body, and my choice would determine the number of 'journeys' I would have to make. I opted for the couple which seemed to me the most adequate to fulfil my future work. The man and the woman were young, in love.

'Those are the ones', I said.

All the consequences of my choice, all the traps that would be set to trip me up, all the paths which my free will would have to choose between were then revealed to me. And when my decision was registered, a luminous shaft of light burst from my being in the woman's direction. I was thrown, precipitated at incredible speed towards the earth, a move which was accompanied by a growing pain, for from the ethereal substance that I was – diffuse and diaphanous – I began to become concentrated and solidified. At the very moment I touched the target, the fire of a masculine sex, which was my father's, cut in me in two as the blade of a sword would and I lost consciousness, pierced by a terrible pain.

This vision came to me when I was seven years old, at an age when I was completely ignorant of anything to do with physical love and procreation. The effect it had on me was considerable. When I woke up, I wept desperately, for I realized that birth had made me an incomplete being. When my father divided me into two, I had lost the other half of myself. I was born a man, and the woman that I also was was missing. I understood gradually that on the other side of the barrier we are all androgynous in the image of God who has no sex and who cannot be conceived as sexed. The curse of the process of earthly incarnation is being separated from one's double. Since then, I have come to perceive, in a somewhat confused manner, that the duality which I had discerned in the world was a misleading semblance and that wholeness was the primordial state which must be reconquered. We have been one in the peace of God and we experience today the painful feeling of being dispersed. We each have been an immaterial soul and are today a prisoner of the flesh.

Each man and each woman carries in them their feminine or masculine double. Wholeness is hidden deep inside us. That is why the alchemist says: 'Descend into your entrails as Orpheus into hell to find Euridice, like Dante seeking Beatrice, and you will become complete, a Janus, a crowned king–queen, you will become the sacred androgyne and you will be one with God. *Visita interiora terrae et invenies occultum lapidem*, 'explore the interior of the earth and find the hidden stone'.

That revelation had terrified me. For several days I was ill, incapable of even contemplating others or the world. My situation was all the more difficult to bear because I had no one to confide in. My mother would have just shrugged her shoulders and shaken her head, incredulous. As for my brother, he did not want to hear of it: he, always so practical, so down to earth, considered me an incorrigible dreamer! As we were political refugees, living in a semi-clandestine way, I had no companions, although I did go to school. But character and necessity kept me away from the others. The atmosphere of permanent denunciation which reigned in those troubled times recommended prudence. Besides, my grandmother, who knew the science of dream interpretation warned me:

'Be careful. If you have secrets, keep them well guarded, above all don't tell anyone.'

But, sometimes, I had trouble containing myself. Therefore, when my little sister said she was born in a rose and my brother in a cabbage, it happened that I went into a terrific rage and I surprised my mother by declaring with conviction,

'I knocked on your door and said: "Woman from this day on, you will be my mother".'

For I was conscious of having chosen her before being born. She was my mother, not by chance, but because I had wished it to be so. I loved her all the more for it. Doubly so because my father's death had condemned her to a most cruel solitude.

Being solitary myself, deprived of a friendly ear, I often went to the seaside or lost myself in the forest where I stayed for a long time, listening to the breeze ruffling the leaves. I was in love with the wind. Storms delighted me. I use to leave the house furtively. I submitted to the winds and ran on the moors, facing the sky while the wind filled me with its power. Nature's violence fascinated me and the unruliness of the elements seemed to reinforce my own energy.

In those moments of communion with nature, my solitude no longer weighed upon me. I spent hours sitting on rocks, contemplating the sea, listening to the crashing of the waves which echoed the movements of my soul. Entranced, I often forgot the passing of the hours.

'Where have you been?' asked my mother when I finally returned.

'I was looking at the sea.'

'Oh, you will never change!' she said.

The earth, which the Greeks named Gaia, has always seduced me. Dare I confess that it is to Gaia that I owe my first amorous experience? On a summer's day, at the age of 12, I felt an urgent need to make love. While on the moor, in Brittany, I dug a hole in the humus, buried my sex in it, and with abrupt thrusts pressed and pressed. At the moment when I inseminated the earth a flash of lightning passed before my eyes, the earth shook and I fell, inebriated by the smell of heather, rush and gorse.

Since that symbolic union, I feel that Gaia loves me, protects and warns me. Every time I travelled to India, for example, there was this unbearable heat, the air was charged with nauseating smells and the earth trembled. It was Gaia whispering to me:

'Go back on your tracks, you're not from here. There are other countries.'

On the other hand, when I set foot for the first time on Egyptian soil, the earth vibrated, as if to tell me: 'At last, you have come again.'

The same thing happened in Guadalupe, in Japan and in Mexico.

The earth is a mother to me. She gave me life. This bond which many people have lost, I feel in every fibre of my being. I feel the telluric forces, the knots where the ground's energy is active, the places I should go to and those I should keep away from. If I am walking in the forest with friends and we get lost, instinctively I point to the right direction. Wherever I go, Gaia guides my steps.

At school, I felt inclined towards subjects related to Gaia. I showed a greater aptitude for the subjects which had to do with the earth, natural sciences, drawing and above all history and geography. I was in the group of pupils who were head of the class.

Yet my mother did not push me to study. She gave us – myself, my brother and my sisters – total freedom, asking only that we show her respect, especially regarding our presence in the house at regular hours. She never asked what we did at school, did not supervise our homework and did not want to sign our notebook showing our school marks. We were to do it ourselves. When the teachers distributed the much feared notebooks, we signed them immediately under the astonished eyes of our young colleagues who trembled at the idea of the beating they would get from their fathers. The headmaster asked my mother to come and speak to him on the subject.

'It's inadmissible!' he said, indignant. 'Your children signed their marks notebooks themselves!'

'That's right', my mother replied from the height of her Spanish pride. 'What is wrong with that? After all, it is they who are responsible for their studies, not me. I could not care less about their studies. If they want to become tramps, they will be tramps. If they want to become ministers, they will be ministers. I don't want to bother with that. It is up to them to know what they want to make of their lives.'

That feigned indifference was in fact the best encouragement. Out of pride and to show that we were capable of doing well, but also not to disappoint a mother who, in spite of what she said, made sacrifices to pay for our studies, we were always among the first in our class. I remember that my mother repeated:

'You study for yourselves! If one day you are successful you will owe it to yourselves and not to me.'

But academic work was not the only reason for my success in passing my exams at the end of secondary school, some years later. When I turned 14, we left Morlaix to settle in Sables d'Olonne – where we weren't to stay for very long. Opposite our house there was a holiday camp and the woman in charge was an old Russian lady who the neighbours thought a bit crazy, because she was passionate about spiritualism. One day, as I passed her in the street, she stopped me:

'You! Come here! What's your name? I feel that you are a great medium. We should try a little experiment together.'

Some time later, intrigued, I knocked on her door. She looked harmless enough, that old lady, but out of prudence and wanting to avoid any tricks, I made a bargain with her:

'I'm willing to do the medium experiment with you . . . but only on one condition! It is that we do it in full daylight, with open windows.'

'As you wish, my child!'

We settled in front of a screen. Imitating the old lady, I opened my fingers wide, some centimetres above a table. We were alone, the windows wide open, in a room flooded with light. Silent, we concentrated for a moment. And suddenly there was a great jolt, I saw the table move and then rise up in the air! I immediately bent over to look underneath, thinking to find some trickery. Nothing! The screen was levitating above the floor. I began to realize that I had made it move. Something took hold of me and I made the table turn. All excitement, the old lady cried:

'You are an incredible medium. I have never seen anything like it. You have an extraordinary power in your hands!'

As I left, she added: 'Try and use it well'.

Two years later, I was to use that power to pass my baccalauréat (secondary school final exams). Under the pretext that I had missed too many classes due to our move and that I was not up to it, the headmaster of the Sable d'Olonne lycée was against my taking the exams. Determined to have a go at it, I decided to overlook his recommendation. One week before the exams, I did a session of spiritualism and asked the table:

'What will be the subjects for the baccalauréat exams?'

I patiently noted all the letters dictated by the table: one knock for A, two for B, and so on. So having obtained the information on the subjects, I plunged into an 'enlightened' study, passed with flying colours and obtained my diploma!

When I was 17, encouraged by a school friend, I went up to Paris and registered with the Académie des Beaux Arts where I would spend ten years studying architecture.

Before long I was making use of my mediumistic talents to astonish my companions. Often, to amuse the crowd in the clubs of Saint-Germain, I played at making the table turn. I asked somebody to write down a few words on a piece of paper and using the table as intermediary, according to the numbers of knocks obtained, I found out what the sentence was. This was not done in the calm shadowy atmosphere of a library but in chaotic conditions, while people danced be-bop!

Nevertheless, I took care not to abuse my powers. First of

all, because those sessions cost me a colossal amount of energy, but also because an inner voice warned:

'Stop! You are wasting your vitality and you may well pay for it, one day.'

I also had the feeling I was playing with fire. Yet, all the time I was practising my tricks, I considered that my power was nothing surprising nor in the least supernatural. I even found all kinds of perfectly rational and credible explanations for it. I believed, and still do, that every human being emits waves in space – 'thought-waves' or 'egregious thought' (of a more collective nature). Perhaps because I was endowed with a somewhat unusual sensitivity, I could get hold of those thought-waves, intercept them and, therefore, retranscribe them, rather like the antennae of radio stations receive radio-electric waves. In conclusion, I was only exploiting the capac-ities of the human body, capacities which my colleagues had 'forgotten' how to develop. It was a precious gift, in the same way that others can possess, for example, perfect pitch. But I soon became conscious that this faculty could reveal itself as extremely dangerous for one endowed with it.

As a student of architecture, I found myself in the work-shop of Auguste Perret, the inventor of reinforced concrete. Our teachers thought that our apprenticeship should encom-pass a thorough knowledge of the world around us. Consequently we had the privilege, thanks to their initiative, to travel abroad on several occasions.

In May 1955 we went to Poland. It was just at the end of the post-war period and Warsaw was still being rebuilt. The Polish capital was buried under scaffolding, as were the towns of Cracow and Zakopane where we felt as though we were crossing vast building sites. Then came the inevitable visit to Auschwitz. Accompanied by an old Polish guide, our group alighted from the old bus at some distance from the camp. It was a beautiful day, a light wind brought the song of the skylark hidden in the rustling corn. We reached the gates. I trailed at the back, without quite knowing why, incapable of sharing my companions' carefree attitude as they talked animatedly, clicking away with their cameras.

As soon as I crossed the threshold of the barbed wire enclosure a heavy silence compressed my ear drums. A silence which I alone seemed conscious of. Leaving my companions to continue, I retraced my steps and as I did so, I could again hear the wind in the wheat, the song of the skylarks in the distance. I went once again back into Auschwitz. Absolute silence. Deadly silence. Distraught, I began invoking God – a God of which I had but a rather vague idea, a humanity-God of whom I begged forgiveness: 'Forgive us, my God, for all the crimes which man may have committed!' I felt guilty, as if by the simple fact of being a man myself, I shared in the responsibility for those atrocities.

At the time Auschwitz had not yet been transformed into an austere museum and one could still see there some horrible remains – covers woven with women's hair, soaps made of human fat. I found myself in the hearth of abomination, in 'Seth's furnace'. The tiniest stone, the slightest object weighed a ton, leadened, imbued with the weight of cruelty and undeserved suffering. Matter no longer emitted sounds which were audible to me. That horror oppressed me and the further in I went, almost staggering, the more I hung on to prayer as though to a life-saving raft. I screamed inwardly: 'Forgive! My God! Forgive! For all that we have subjected our brothers to, forgive us!'

Following in the steps of our Polish guide, my companions started going down the ramp which led to the crematoriums. In Auschwitz, these installations were buried under the ground. I stayed back, deep in my prayers. My comrades penetrated with the guide into the dark underground tunnel. They seemed barely conscious of the place they were entering, whistling, their hands in their pockets, cameras on their shoulders. They disappeared and, afraid of losing them, I rushed to join them, running down the ramp, when suddenly I received a blow on my chest, a violent shock which stopped me in my tracks. At that moment I saw a hand emerge from the void, a hand without a body which pushed me back up to the top of the ramp.

Bewildered, I intensified my prayers. I wanted to deny that force and to resist. I started down again, but untiringly the hand took me back to my point of departure. I was afraid I might lose sight of my companions at the moment when I needed their presence most. Suddenly, I saw them coming out by another ramp, some distance away from where I was. The hand disappeared at once. Skirting the obstacle, I rejoined the group which had scarcely noticed my absence. I revealed nothing of what had happened, I even tried to hide my indescribable state of confusion. They would not have understood, and would perhaps even have laughed at me. My story would have seemed ridiculously pious to those free thinkers.

Later, I understood that all those people, the old men and women, the initiates, those women and children who died in the underground gas chambers had, in their last breath, cursed humanity for the suffering which was imposed on them. And since that time, there has been a guardian of the threshold watching over that site. He let my friends through, but he found a way of telling me:

'No, you will not go down!'

Possessing mediumistic faculties and being deep in prayer, it was dangerous for me to enter that gas chamber. I would have been hit by the terrifying screams of those men and women which could have obliterated me. Therefore the guardian of the threshold forbade me access. Far from rejecting me, he was offering me his protection.

I spent the following night praying, asking God to forgive men for all the hideous crimes committed, for as a human being I am simultaneously victim and executioner. I feel both the fault and the pain inflicted. That visit to Auschwitz was a turning point in my life. The death camp seemed a sign announcing the apocalypse, a stage of that destructive folly which seems to animate human beings.

My time at the Beaux Arts school was an essential phase from all points of view. Professionally, of course, even if I was to opt for a different path later, but also personally, for I pursued my personal inner researches, studying and reading avidly. I confirmed my gifts as a medium and while identifying the scenarios of my waking dreams, I was comforted by the idea that I had lived previous lives and that there was a permanent 'me', eternal, which did not restrict itself to the present incarnation, but which I did not yet dare to call my 'self' or my 'soul'.

I also met friends whose influence was very important for my spiritual evolution, in particular a friend whose father was an Egyptologist and who had been brought up by two great magicians, Aor and Isha. He lent me their books and I met the 'children of Aor' in Grasse on the Côte d'Azur. They were exceptional beings, and thanks to them I began, little by little, to progress in the path of knowledge.

My 'privileged' relationship with the other world, the impalpable world, continued to reveal itself to me, sometimes in extremely violent ways, as if to call me back to order, as well as to tell me not to lose track of what is essential.

I was at an age when lovesickness often overrules other preoccupations. There again, I was something of an outsider. But this was far from being an enviable position, even causing me to feel deep shame. At the age of 26, I was still a virgin. At the time, to make such a confession would have been highly embarrassing for me. I was a virgin because physical love did not interest me. My companions' licentious behaviour and debauchery scared me and filled me with disgust. I felt a revulsion for the purely physical bestial act. I hoped for an ideal harmony with the person I would meet. I wanted a mystical union – a fusion of beings. I had mad, immoderate dreams like most young people. It's possible that I was following my mother's example, who having been madly in love with my father, remained faithful to his memory after his death, which occurred when she was merely 29 years old. Like her, I dreamed of a unique love.

When I was 26, I fell madly in love for the first time, with someone at the Beaux Arts. But to my great despair, our relationship was strictly on a basis of friendship. As my desire grew I decided to act, that is, to put my powers to the test. I lived, at the time, in the attic at 73 Hausmann Boulevard, in an austere student's room, sparsely furnished with an iron bed, a table and a chair. My mother occupied a neighbouring room. Shut in my den, I fashioned a wax doll. Inside it I placed a photo of my beloved and a lock of hair, then for several days I focused on it!

'I want you to love me, I want you to love me', I repeated with passion.

One night, as I was going to bed, I was amazed to notice that a slight phosphorescence emanated from the statuette. It shone in the room's shadowy light. I stood there looking at it, asking myself if I wasn't the victim of some optical illusion. But during the days that followed, there was no longer any doubt possible: the intensity of that phosphorescence had gone on increasing.

I was impressed by the extent of my powers. The results were soon to become evident. The person in question started paying attention to me. I had been successful! Fascinated by the power that I could exert over another human being, I continued my practices.

One night when there was a full moon, I woke up with a jolt, feeling a presence in the room. Yet I was sure I had locked the door and no thief could enter by the roof, for there were bars on the windows. I saw no one in the room. It was empty, lit by the rays of the moon. But suddenly the springs of my bed started to creak. Someone had just sat beside me! There on the mattress I clearly saw, just by my thigh, the imprint of a body! I sat up at once, absolutely terrified. That invisible being held my hands firmly, pressing my wrists. Soon I felt breath on my face, then it was a cheek which pressed against mine. I had the impression that the person wanted to get into me to possess my soul. I withdrew from that horrible embrace, violently rejecting the intruder with my two out-stretched hands and hugging the wall, possessed by a vivid terror.

All night I fought with the invisible. A hundred times I thought I would lose my reason. If it were not for those bars on the windows, I would have thrown myself out into the void to end that unequal combat.

At dawn, the 'thing' disappeared as suddenly as it had come. Shortly afterwards, my mother brought me my break-fast. She found me in an alarming state:

'What is the matter with you? You look green!'

'It's nothing', I lied. 'I slept badly. I must have eaten some-thing which did not go down too well.'

She did not insist. As soon as I was alone again, I jumped up, took the wax statuette and dissolved it in hot water. Then I went and threw the photo and the lock of hair into the Seine. Afterwards I went on a round of all the churches in Paris to light a candle, saying in each one:

'Forgive me, my God, for what I was doing . . . '

I felt I had done wrong: I had wanted to play at being a sor-cerer's apprentice. I had given myself over to a devilish act and someone had been sent from above to wake me up, to warn me not to lose my soul. It was the first time in my life – and the last – that I burned my wings.

This episode, which luckily had no malevolent conse-quences, had a great impact on me. I stopped using my medium-istic gifts for any purposes which might serve my ego. But, above all, I became conscious that the powers with which I was endowed and which, up to that time, I had explained away, under the influence of my mother's materialistic thinking, by attributing them to an 'extraordinary' sensorial sensibility, were, in fact, of a superior, divine origin. The notion of God, which I had already sensed at Auschwitz, came up again within me. But it did not yet impose itself. On the contrary, I needed new manifestations to believe:

'My God, if You really exist, I pray that You show Yourself!'

The absolute pride of the Pharisee who demands a sign from God to believe! But from then on, night and day, I prayed fervently. I prayed from the moment I woke in the morning, I prayed on my way to the Beaux Arts or when drawing up plans on my drawing board. I invoked God while eating and when walking the streets of Paris.

'God, if You exist, show Yourself! I am here, I am waiting for a sign from You.'

And while I walked sparks flashed from the ground, hitting my left heel. But for me, it was still a manifestation of my mediumistic powers. Likewise, when I entered a church, the old sculpted wood creaked when I passed.

One day I was on the Metro, on the Mairie-des-Lilas-Châtelet line, alone on the last coach, praying:

'My God, if You exist, show Yourself.'

And suddenly, there was an explosion. A huge detonation. Whatever it was, the glass of the carriage had imploded and the chips reassembled in a ball at my feet! Just a simple accident? I have never found an explanation for it. Shocked, I could only think of one thing: if by chance the inspector came, I would be accused of vandalism! But how could one explain that the glass had burst inwards and not outwards?

As soon as the train stopped at the Place-des-Fêtes station, I ran as fast as I could. I ran until I dropped from exhaustion. Then, recovering my breath with difficulty, I meditated on what had just happened. A message had been sent to me with the following meaning: prayer was not something that emanated from me to rise towards the cosmos. On the contrary, prayer was a kind of black hole which attracted energies. I was myself a black hole, a parcel and a replica of the cosmos and my powers found their origin in this oneness with the whole. God would not come to me, I would elevate myself towards Him, when I was strong enough.

Some weeks later, one Sunday in September, I went to the Pershing stadium in Vincennes, near the racecourse, to meet a friend who played football. It was a greyish day and a fine drizzle battered my face. The dreary weather did not stop the players running from one end of the pitch to the other. I watched, standing at the edge of the pitch, for there were neither steps nor benches to sit on. As I followed the match, rather distracted, I prayed, faithful to my habit. Suddenly, the rain stopped. An immense rainbow pierced the clouds and spanned the pitch. An arch of alliance, linking the sky and the earth, formed before me.

As I contemplated this spectacle with delight, I felt projected towards a dazzling light, very high in the cosmos. The world around me had disappeared. There were no more football players or pitch. I was alone faced with that prodigious light which radiated goodness, truth and justice and conveyed to me the unthinkable, the unbelievable which I still feel today in the smallest fibre of my being: eternity. I was eternal within eternity. I knew that powerful, sublime and ineffable joy which abolishes barriers. I was the infinitude of my being, experiencing in myself the unity of the cosmos and the unfolding in all things of the supreme energy.

A millionth of a second later, I found myself back on the football pitch, my feet on the wet grass. I had just known eternity. I stood there, completely overwhelmed and dumbfounded. I told the friend I had come to see that I felt slightly dizzy and needed to go for a walk.

'Go by car with the others', I told him. 'Don't worry about me. I am going to walk home, it will do me good.'

It had started to rain again. In this drenching drizzle I made my way back to Paris, slowly, along the edge of the Bois de Vincennes, still dazzled, but with my spirit full of questions.

'What happened?' I kept asking myself. 'It's not possible! I can't have seen God! It's fabulous, unbelievable!'

As I walked, my rationalist side began to take over again. My brain exuded a musty Cartesian smell.

'You're delirious! You have prayed like a fanatic every day for three years and you've just been through the most hysterical of scenes! Freud must be hooting with laughter in his grave.'

But what I had just experienced was so beautiful, so pure, my soul was still feeling so happy, enlightened by that eternity which I had felt, that I could not decide what the exact nature of that event was. You can easily imagine my confusion.

Deep in thought, I continued to walk by the Seine, in the direction of Charenton. I crossed over to the left bank, went through the Gare d'Austerlitz and along the Jardin des Plantes. I finally arrived behind Notre-Dame, on the embankment where the second-hand booksellers are to be found. But on this rainy Sunday the place was deserted.

And then suddenly, somebody in front of me called out: 'Monsieur!'

I lifted my eyes and saw a man dressed entirely in black. 'Here', he said to me.

And he put into my hands an old leather-bound book. I lifted the cover and read: *Mysterium Magnum*, by Jakob Böeme. I closed the book and went to thank my generous benefactor, but . . . there was no one there! He had disappeared! I looked around . . . the embankment was deserted! Then, I understood, God had sent me a messenger. Furious at my denial of the evidence, irritated by my invocation of a hysterical crisis, He had materialized someone who had come to me with this book, as if to say: 'You want material evidence, well, here it is!' Jakob Böeme, whose books I soon devoured, had been a 17th-century cobbler, a mystic who, after an enlightenment, wrote what could certainly be considered some of the most beautiful pages on God.

Because it swept away my last materialistic doubts, that day remains a cornerstone for me. Since then, I can say that I really have a strong, well-rooted faith. It has become, therefore, as impossible for me to doubt the existence of God as it is to deny my faith in Him. After having 'felt' eternity and this materialization from the 'other side', I could no longer refuse myself to God.

That materialization was not the last. Some years later, I had a similar experience, at a moment when I was in great danger, not spiritual danger, but physical. In 1968, I went to Japan for the first time. I was invited to present my haute couture collection, having been a fashion designer since 1964. After Japan, I decided to make my way back to France with some friends, stopping all over Asia. We came back via Hong Kong, Taiwan, Cambodia and Thailand and I very much wanted to visit the great Khmer temple of Angkor Vat.

When we arrived at Phnom Penh, we took a small plane which took us up to Angkor Vat where we landed as the sun reached its zenith. During that month of August the heat was suffocating and it overwhelmed us as soon as we set foot on the tarmac which was steaming. When we arrived at the King's Hostel, a seedy hotel which owes its clientele solely to the fact that it is in the vicinity of the temple, we had a quick lunch and everybody declared that they were ready to have a siesta. The guide said: 'Around six o'clock, when the sun is setting, we will go and visit Angkor.'

I was not enthusiastic about this plan. I sleep very little and I found the idea of a siesta boring. Therefore, I decided to go and visit the temple alone. To get there I had to follow a paved street a kilometre long with ditches on both sides. I started walking, perceiving in the distance the towers of that extraordinary temple, one of the most beautiful human constructions, on a par with the Egyptian pyramids.

I made my way at a leisurely pace. The scorching sun was overwhelming and slowing me down and there was no breeze to lighten that burning air which enveloped and asphyxiated me. Suddenly, having walked three-quarters of the way, I felt the blood vessels of my nose burst. The blood started pouring abundantly onto my lips, then between my fingers. My head started to spin and it felt as if it was being crushed in a vice. The earth beneath my feet began to waver. It was as if all my strength had left me. I could neither go forwards nor back.

'My God', I thought, 'How stupid to be walking in such heat, without protection for my head. I probably have sunstroke. I am going to die like an idiot . . . away from home.'

At that moment a child's chuckle, a mocking laugh, echoed in the hot mist which held me hostage. I looked in the direction of the temple and saw that, perched on a stone under the large porch, there was a young monk, aged around 14 or 15, draped in an orange cloth, his head shaved. Sitting cross-legged he was holding his sides and laughing at me. His wide smile underlined his high cheekbones and made wrinkles in his eyelids, under which I imagined there must be black, brilliant eyes like lead marbles. Annoyed to hear him mocking me openly, I found the strength to stand up and start to walk again. Staggering, I managed to reach the shade of the porch and leant against the stone, exhausted. After half-an-hour I had recovered and the blood had stopped pounding in my ears but the young monk had disappeared. I searched everywhere in that vast temple, visiting the galleries, crossing large rooms looking for the young monk who, inadvertently, has just saved my life, but Angkor Vat was absolutely deserted. There was no one there.

I gave up and decided to return to the hotel. Once there, I asked our guide:

'Tell me, the monks who go to that temple . . .' I started to say.

'What monks are you talking about?' he replied. 'That is an abandoned temple, no monks ever go there.' I stood there, astounded. I was sure I had not dreamed the incident! The monk had not been a mirage, but a live being of flesh and blood! I understood then that the heavens had sent down a child to save my life. My destiny was not to die at Angkor Vat on that particular day.

Every time my life has been in peril, each time I've had to make important decisions or confront difficult trials, the heavens have sent some sign to direct me, to guide me or put me on my guard. Now, when the heavens or destiny send such signs or trials, one's view of the world is thereby completely changed and one begins to ask oneself essential questions. All of a sudden, one becomes aware that the 'real' world, the material world in which we live, is but a kind of illusion. There is a higher reality behind the scene, a primordial reality which we, sometimes, get a glimpse of.

We are often like those prisoners which Plato speaks of, prisoners who at the deep end of a cavern, turn their back on the light and only recognize objects through their projected shadow. But, luckily, we are not condemned to live in that ignorant state for life. The world which surrounds us is full of signs which we must learn to unravel. Of all the arts, it is, without doubt, poetry which is the most conscious of this phenomenon. Therefore, Baudelaire alerted us ceaselessly to the 'correspondence' between heaven and earth:

> Nature is a temple where live pillars
> Utter perchance confused words
> Man wanders there through a forest of symbols
> Which observe him with a familiar gaze

The other world, the world 'beyond', gives us little signs which, for one who knows, discloses its presence everywhere. That path is not reserved for 'initiates'. Or rather, each person can become an initiate, for an initiate is precisely that, one who starts to follow the path of knowledge. I do not possess a particular truth, I am not a prophet, I do not propose any system or dogma. But I am a witness and I would like to share my experience and perhaps incite other people to explore their inner life as well as to progress towards the light.

I kept silent for a long time, for I thought I was alone and I feared ridicule. I often asked myself:

'Why me? What have I done to deserve those signs from heaven? What have I done to deserve this sensorial acuity which draws me closer to the divine? Why have I kept the memory of my previous lives?'

But as the years went by, I met a multitude of people who told me that they had had similar experiences. If they did not speak about them openly, it was because they feared they would be considered mad or as people who hung on to the 'beyond' because their life was a failure, or even taken for charlatans who want to shine in society. Therefore, I waited until I had attained a certain success and become well known, in short, until I had nothing to prove, to tell my story and present it as it really is: a personal adventure and a 'feeling' which I have no intention of turning into a doctrine.

My only ambition is to encourage people to open their eyes. The world in which we live is not the only reality. Our passage on earth is not the totality of our life. There is another vision of the world. There is a sublime, infinite world which extends the frontiers of knowledge.

If I had a message, it would be the following: 'Beware! What you see down here is not all there is. The rest is available to you if you take the trouble to find out, if you know how to find the keys. For those keys are not beyond your reach: we carry them in ourselves'. That is the recommendation found in the alchemists' **VITRIOL** – *Visita interiora terrae rectificando invenies occultum lapidem* – 'explore your entrails and you will find the hidden stone'.

2

The Veil of Isis

The visible world is a symbol of the invisible world
JAKOB BÖEME

If the quest for the self and what is beyond the visible world is open to each and everyone, it is none the less a long and difficult road. In effect the knowledge is concealed or secret, hidden like the face of the goddess Isis, behind a veil. That veil is first of all the material world with its deceitful appearances which hide the essential from us. The bodies, the forms and the substances are so many smoke curtains which cover up divine mysteries. But the veil of Isis can also be those passions which mislead us, making us lose our way in pursuit of vain objectives, such as money, power or social success. Illusions which make us fall into the trap of materialism are attractive delusions which distract us from the real goal. We spend our time chasing dreams and worshipping the 'golden calf'. Isis' veil is also all the weight of our social life with all it entails: conformity, false opinions and prejudices, ignorance, superstition and fear.

The first step in the quest for the self consists in becoming free of all prejudices and of everything that is imposed by outer rules. This does not mean living like a recluse, but one must continuously learn to look at the world in a new way. At the beginning of this chapter I would ask no more of the reader than that he listens to what I have to say and that he be attentive to nature's signals! He can then form his own opinion freely.

As for me, I was lucky not to be imprisoned by any form of dogma. The opposition which existed between my Marxist mother and my Catholic grandmother saved me from any monolithic thinking. Because I loved both of them with the same passion, one could not be more right than the other. My love was able to conciliate every antagonism. In fact these differences of opinion instilled in me, at an early age, a certain openness of spirit and tolerance, as well as giving me a taste for observation and reflection. For Isis' veil is not opaque. It lets precious messages filter through. But we must be vigilant, otherwise, as the Bible says: *'They will have eyes to see and they will not see. They will have ears to hear, but they will not hear.'*

A curious child, I never tired of observing the world. One thing perplexed me. The Marxist theory which I was taught at home professed that men are born equal, but that they are later privileged or handicapped by their social, economic and family environment. Now, this theory did not coincide with what I could observe around me. And I did not have to look very far. In my family, my brother and my two sisters, although submitted to the same exterior conditions as myself, were all extremely different. Made from the same mould, brought up according to the same model, we showed aptitudes and inclinations which were completely disparate. What an abyss between my brother and myself! He, always so materialistic, so dynamic, and I, such a dreamer, so introverted. How could we understand the world in such radically opposed ways?

This was an insoluble enigma for me. In spite of all that my mother taught me, I verified every day that there were considerable differences between each individual, in the bosom of the same family circle. Consequently there must be something other than a simple social or atavistic determinism. I found the beginning of a solution to that problem with my waking dreams and my first astral voyage experiences. These illuminations revealed to me that the 'difference', that basic foundation of my own self, could be explained by the fact that I had lived other lives, that I came from a distant past, although this was still a vague notion. Logically, I was driven to conclude that my brother and my sisters came from completely different horizons. From then on, everything became clearer to me. If the members of the same family appear to be so 'heterogeneous', if their destinies are so strikingly different, it is because they follow different paths which suddenly cross at the same point in time and space. They are like travellers who, although they don't have the same destination, are reunited aboard the same ship and will travel together part of the way.

Apart from these different itineraries and the consequent multiplicity of characters which ensued, I found further signs of these differences in the physical particularities to which my grandmother paid great attention. She thought that every hidden characteristic would be reflected in an individual's face or in his attitude. The visible world contained a hidden message. One had to surpass the formal appearance, lift the corner of the veil to find the deeper meaning. I started to observe people with great attention, studying their hands, the shape of the ears, deciphering their faces. Proceeding from a hypothesis, I tried to find universal rules, to establish parallels between the physical and the mental or the spiritual. In fact, I was practising physiognomy without knowing it.

I paid special attention to the ears, attributing to them a privileged value: do their shape not remind one of a foetus bent over itself, upside down? I found that some people have ear lobes that are attached to their head, or sometimes they are non-existent, whereas others have a very developed lobe (see p. 38). I tried, by a simple empirical method, to attribute a value to that difference which could not be just chance, for in the same family, among people who had the same genetic code, one found astonishing disparities. At the lycée, the more domineering, pushy and quarrelsome among my companions, those who were most in the grip of material reality, all had very reduced ear lobes, whereas those who were introverted, thoughtful, more intellectual or dreamers had very well-developed lobes. The former possessed animal aggression and it showed in the form of their ear. I concluded that this was their first life, whereas the others had already lived many lives and were, therefore, more spiritually attuned.

Oriental iconography later confirmed my deductions: I was not surprised to find that the Buddha, the immortal sage, was always represented with excessively long ear lobes, which almost came down to his shoulders. And is it not said that Lao-tsu, the founder of Taoism, had ears which were seven inches long, earning him the nickname 'long-ears'? Was this perhaps a reference to the faculty of listening to the 'inner self' and of hearing the vibrations which animate all that lives and breathes?

In the same way the hand is very revealing. There is no need to know the secrets of its lines to perceive how much it can betray someone's feelings or personality. When I first started observing hands, I came upon a mystery. I was astonished to find women with men's hands and vice versa. I also frequently saw huge people with tiny children's hands and very thin people with large, bony hands. Not only were the hands often not in harmony with the rest of the body, they often did not correspond to the person's chosen profession. There were pianists with thick, peasant hands and, the reverse, road workers with long pianist phalanxes. What was the hidden message behind all these 'anomalies'?

I considered this in terms of the hypothesis that we preserve physical signs of our past lives. Hands seemed very important to me, for after all they are the instruments of our actions, the extension of our thoughts. The thumb symbolizes man and the fingers are the four elements which protect him. Therefore, the child comes into the world with the thumb held in by the four fingers and the old man preparing to die closes his hand instinctively over his thumb.

And why do smokers find it so difficult to let go of their cigarette? It is said, with reason, that it gives them composure. Many people do not know what to do with their hands. They always need to cross and uncross their arms, showing embarrassment, holding them on their chest or massaging mechanically the inside of their palm or playing with their ring. At the Beaux Arts I observed, amused, the gesticulation of my teachers on their podium. When they noticed I was observing them, they became disconcerted, suddenly conscious of their hands. They then grabbed a ruler or a pencil to tap on the desk. It is as if people become aware that a deeper part of their being is thus revealed and becomes evident in spite of their efforts.

Dynamic people always have their thumb pushed out; they assert their personalities before others; they express their generosity. On the other hand, the timid ones, the introverted, always have their thumb folded in, protected by their fingers, for they are afraid to express themselves.

I also became aware that people with small hands are those who require a great deal of attention, who like to be counselled and supported, spoilt. Those with large hands, on the contrary, are very independent and have strong characters; they find it difficult to bear other people's interference. Little by little, I understood that one preserved from previous lives, the size of one's hands. Small hands belong to those who, in previous lives, died during childhood or adolescence, who need to be emotionally comforted or sexually dominated, whereas large hands denote maturity on the part of a person and more autonomy, no doubt one who died at an advanced age. That kind of individual does not, in general, seek physical contact.

I also managed to establish several 'types' of hand. Among others, there are those with veins which show on the surface, pertaining to men of action, soldiers and explorers. There are intellectual hands or those of the common people. Then there are the round hands, without muscles, like mine, that are the hands of priests and men of faith. I have always had the feeling that I had lived many lives as a priest, in places like Egypt or during the Inquisition. These remarks are, obviously, in no way scientific. But perhaps you would grant me the benefit of the doubt, and if you study these things for yourself you will see that there is something to it.

Another basically revealing feature is the eye. One knows that iridology claims to be able to determine, by examining the iris, the nature and the seat of certain troubles or physical lesions. During the last century, the forensic police even believed that they could find in the pupil of a victim a 'photograph' of his assassin. But the global aspect of the eye is a rich source of many other types of information.

Women have always known the importance of the eyes, making up their eyelashes and their eyelids to send men messages. When I was a child, the fashion was to have almond-shaped eyes. Women used to draw fawn-shaped eyes or cat's eyes to say to their partner 'I am a feline, a sensual woman'. It was a kind of code. To generalize further, one could say that people with slanted eyes, eyes that go upwards towards the temples (and almost non-existent ear lobes) are seductive, sensorial. They bite into life with vigour, often burning the candle at both ends. They are active and intemperate. I have had the opportunity to verify that people who excel in excessively physical professions such as soldiers, policemen or professional sportspeople tend to have these outer characteristics, whereas those who have horizontal eyes (and long ear lobes) are temperate people, introverted, almost jostled by life and who dislike violent action. The more the eye is on a horizontal line, the greater the introversion and the reflection.

36

I soon came to the conclusion that, in our evolution, we progressively leave the animal state to accede to our humanity, but we keep certain traits of our previous state. At birth, in our first life, we have animal eyes and as we go through our successive reincarnations we arrive at the horizontal eye, which I call the eye of Christ. Refining my observations over the years, I noted that, among people who have horizontal eyes, it is possible to distinguish several stages. Those whose iris is placed low, still covered in part by the lower lid, are those who can count the lesser number of lives. The iris is like a sun and indicates the age of our soul. When it is placed well at the centre of the eye, the person is well advanced and has only a few lives left to live. When the upper lid covers the upper iris, we have reached the setting sun, that is to say the last earthly incarnation.

Passionate about drawing and believing that all that is observable is symbolic and vice versa, I was able to collect a certain number of signs which came to confirm my belief in the survival of the soul and in its successive reincarnations. Today, when I find myself face to face with someone, I cannot help but observe their hands, the shape of their ears, the inclination of their eyes, and the placement of the iris. Immediately I know what to say to them, how to catch their interest, for those characteristics correspond to a deep self, perhaps a non-revealed self; they may well correspond to an unacknowledged self or one that has not yet been recognized in the depth of their being. From then onwards, I start captivating that person, I know what she expects from the world and from others. I perceive that existential restlessness which all beings feel, even the most pragmatic ones. For each one of us, even the most materialistic, carries in some part of his or her self a share of dreams and of the absolute.

All these observations have led me to think that the visible world is not a vain mirage, a worthless illusion that we must distance ourselves from in order to approach truth. By

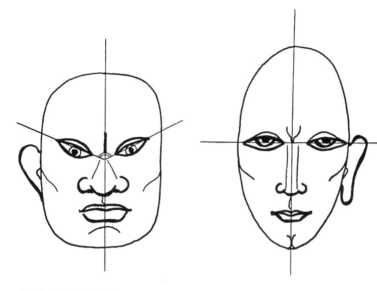

THE FACE OF MATERIALITY

Man leaving animality

Eyes at a sharp angle
Ears without lobes
Active – Material – Sensual

THE FACE OF SPIRITUALITY

Man at the end of reincarnation

Eyes at an angle of 180°
Ears with long lobes
Introverted – Detached – Abstract

READING OF THE NUMBER OF REINCARNATIONS

According to the position of the iris in the eyes at an angle of 180°

Rising sun
Less than 1000 years

Sun at noon
Approximately 2500 years

Setting sun
More than 5000 years

Paco Rabanne 91

38

knowing the exterior, we can come to know the interior and thus guide people, help them to find answers to those questions which they ask themselves. One can also use intuition to have access to the theory of reincarnation. For earthly appearances are not a windshield which cuts us off from a superior reality. Isis' veil masks reality while revealing it and reveals it while masking it.

The signs of reincarnation are not restricted to physical traits. Each of us has experienced those *déjà vu* sensations which one feels when arriving at a place where one has never been before and yet there is a sudden sense of recognition, of having been there before, of having walked on those paving stones, crossed those rooms, contemplated that view in a distant past. Often it is more than a vague impression, for one is able to find one's way, to know about a detail which one could not have had plausible knowledge of. There are innumerable people who, when visiting a town, can say that they have lived in the past in such and such a house and give precise information as to what inscription was engraved on the stone, or that such an event took place there. Where can such knowledge come from? Sometimes it is such a fleeting sensation that we don't have the time to explore it. Or could it be we are perhaps afraid of what we might discover? For there are some truths which cannot be accepted without preparation, some lights which are too blinding to be contemplated when we emerge from obscurity.

The same phenomenon can take place with people. There again, each one of us has had that experience of the 'lightning bolt' effect created by sudden contact with people who we feel as if we have always known, although we are meeting them for the first time. We feel right away that we have affinities with them, things in common. How could I not see in these experiences a sign that we had met before in another life, that we had been close friends or relatives? The reverse can also happen, we may feel an instinctive repulsion for certain people. This may be because they have made us suffer in a past life. They may have robbed, tricked or even killed us. Consequently we refuse to have anything to do with them.

Some years ago, at a dinner, I met three people whom I immediately recognized as being 'friends' or 'brothers', although I had never seen them before. At the first glance we exchanged, it was as if a bolt of lightning had struck us. We all had a sudden illumination, no doubt provoked by our extremely improbable meeting.

I exclaimed: 'We know each other. We were together on a vessel.'

And all three nodded. One of them described the interior of the vessel.

'We come from the planet Altair', I told them. 'I remember that planet which lies at the centre of the galaxy, a crystal planet of extraordinary beauty.'

'Yes', said the third man. 'The seven sages of Cyrius had asked us to travel to earth to verify the progress made by man since his creation a million years ago by the Elohim, the Great Ancients.'

I agreed, 'We arrived on planet earth for the foundation of Atlantis.'

That is how I came to date my oldest memory to approximately 75,000 years before Jesus Christ, a date attributed by Gnosis, the religious science of the adepts, to the creation of Atlantis. Situated to the west of the Iberian Peninsula, the Atlantean civilization possessed the knowledge of the origins, of the 'word' which is lost today. It had attained a high level of social and political organization when it disappeared entirely, engulfed in the space of one day by a gigantic earthquake. It is said that the people of the Basque country are the descendants of the survivors of Atlantis. Their strange language, with no European roots, has always intrigued linguists.

'Birds of a feather flock together' goes the popular saying.

People can be compared to transmitter and receiver mechanisms: they emit a sound wave, a musical note, the volume depending on the development of their mental capacity and according to the number of lives they have already lived. And this is how, instinctively, we are drawn to those who emit energy signals on the same frequency as ours. An 'animalistic', sensorial person, will attract people with a low frequency vibration, who nurture the same desires and have the same preoccupations. The more pure and luminous the sound, the more advanced the people are in their spiritual quest and their desire for communication. We then say that we are 'on the same wavelength'. The discovery of a twin soul never really happens by chance.

Those extraordinary meetings which bring forth a previous life experience from our depths, are extremely rare. More often than not the reminiscence is progressive. When I was a child I would visualize Egyptian scenarios and could not, at the time, identify them. Those still images became animated little by little, the contours became clearer, more coherent, until they formed an understandable story, the complete destiny of a personage which I 'felt' was me, in a body that had been mine. This narrative was confirmed later on during my study of ancient architecture at the Beaux Arts, as it was by my interaction with eminent Egyptologists.

I had been an Egyptian priest officiating in a temple. I initiated pharaohs. I lived side by side with the highest dignitaries of the court of Amenhotep III and I taught the laws of Egypt and its religion to King Amenhotep IV, his son. Abandoning the traditional cult of Amun, the cult of the Ram, Amenhotep IV became a worshipper of the sun, Aten, instituting a monotheistic cult, and took the name of Akhenaten. I felt deep admiration for this sovereign whose reign took place under the sign of great justice. He married Nefertiti, a queen of immense beauty. But, being androgynous like his father, Akhenaten could not fully satisfy the queen's desires. She committed adultery with

Horemheb, captain of all Egyptian armies, who with the help of Amun's clergy – who were furious that the king should have deprived them of their immense power by disowning the cult of Ram – dethroned Akhenaten and abandoned him in the middle of the desert, where he died of exposure.

His young brother then took the title of pharaoh, thus betraying Akhenaten. He officially re-established the cult of the Ram and adopted the name of Toutankhamun. Once Akhenaten was gone, I was forced to make an allegiance with the priests of Amun. They would certainly have preferred to eliminate me, but my rank as high priest initiate rendered me untouchable, and later, with the complicity of twelve priests who had remained faithful to the memory of Akhenaten, I assassinated Toutankhamun soon after his twenty-fourth anniversary. As an embalmer priest, I participated in his embalming and in the enclosure of his body in a funerary chamber – a funerary chamber which the archaeologist Carter discovered in 1922.

When I went to Egypt for the first time, I visited the Cairo museum and there, in those immense dusty rooms, under the somnolent gaze of a guardian, behind those glass showcases, were the vestiges of pharaonic art enveloped in cotton. I felt a terrible shock when I recognized those objects, for I remembered their weight and texture, as if I had manipulated them in a distant and yet incredibly vivid past.

Faced with that accumulation of signs, visions and meetings, which all seemed to indicate that my present life was but a link in a chain of events, whose meaning I could not yet fathom, it is not surprising that I should have taken to the study of ancient history and the history of religions with enthusiasm. I did not always dare to confide in my family or in my companions. I was afraid, as I have already mentioned, of being considered mad or of being thought ridiculous.

And yet what is so ridiculous about believing in the independence and the survival of the soul when faced with those atheists who wanted me to delude myself that this sub-lime principle, this human soul with infinite possibilities, should disappear into nothingness with the putrefaction of my flesh? How could I accept that the creative spirit of men such as Leonardo da Vinci or Mozart is but an assemblage of cells? Is it not more credible to consider that their body was but a receptacle and not the source of their genius?

What is ridiculous about thinking that my soul could return to earth and be reincarnated in a different body? In what way is it more logical to imagine, as was shown by the iconography of a perverted Christianity, that after a brief time on earth – a spark with regard to the universe – I would be judged, admitted into a trite paradise or condemned to roast in an eternal hell? Compared to reincarnation, the dogma of the general resurrection of bodies seemed to me a monstrous aberration. How come? Would a lame person then be reborn lame? A paralysed person disabled?

One may object that it is difficult to admit the idea of re-incarnation if one has no memory of past lives. But do we always remember the first years of our life? Do we keep the memory of all our dreams? And yet both childhood and sleep are integral parts of our existence.

If my studies did not have the same impact on me as those 'deeply felt' experiences, they nevertheless relieved me of my apprehensions by showing me that, far from being a unique case, I had intuitively discovered a belief that is part of humanity's universal heritage. By immersing myself in my reading, I was surprised to discover that most religions on the planet, old and modern, included reincarnation in their doc-trines. The transmigration of souls, also called 'palingenesis' constitutes the very foundation of numerous religions.

My purpose here is not to present an historical or geo-graphical panorama of reincarnation. It suffices to say that the belief in the cyclical materialization of souls is currently admitted by the Orientals, that it is the pillar on which

Hinduism rests and that it is present in the numerous branches of Buddhism and also in Sufism. The majority of ancient civilizations believed in the reincarnation of ancestors, as do numerous so-called primitive peoples. Eminent philosophers and writers, as diverse as Pythagoras, Lao-tsu, Plato, Goethe, Schopenhauer, Flaubert and Thoreau believed in reincarnation. How is it then possible to reject without consideration a belief that is taken as fact by more than half the earth's population? After a long period of ostracism in the West, it is making spectacular progress. Could it be because it responds to our essential preoccupations?

But instead of taking an interest in 'exotic' cultures, we should take a closer look at Christianity, since it is our own universe. The majority of Catholics tend to consider the doctrine of reincarnation as a superstition worthy of a lowly sect or, at best, an oriental curiosity. They imagine that it is contrary to their faith and that it is condemned by the Roman Catholic Church. Nothing could be further from the truth! Strictly speaking, the Catholic religion does not prohibit reincarnation.

The rebirth of souls was considered a real possibility by the early Christians. Then during the 5th and 6th centuries it fell from grace under the influence of a Church attempting to define dogmas which would allow it to fight against heresies, prevent the fragmentation of Christianity and thus allow the clergy to control and maintain a temporal and spiritual power.

At the time of the Fifth Ecumenical Council which took place in Constantinople in the year AD 553, reincarnation was condemned in an arbitrary fashion. This was, moreover, a questionable condemnation, for the bishops chosen by Justinian did not obtain the approval of Pope Vigil. The latter, although in Constantinople, refused to be present at the debates. On the other hand the doctrine of the rebirth of souls was not the object of the Council and its condemnation was obtained indirectly. The fact that the Council of

Constantinople debated the problem of reincarnation should in itself be sufficient proof that this doctrine was very much alive within the early Church. The teaching in question was that of Origenes (AD 185–254), a theologian from Alexandria whom Saint Jerome considered 'the greatest master of the Church, after the apostles'. Origines professed belief in the pre-existence and transmigration of souls.

After the Council of Constantinople, the Church carefully forgot to mention reincarnation. Thus placed under the carpet, this doctrine was soon considered a heresy. It was one of the reasons for the persecution of the Cathars. Let us just recall the meaning of the word 'heretic', an expression covered with such dishonour, such disgrace, that it has almost become synonymous with diabolical. It actually means, etymologically, 'the one who chooses'. Since that time, heretics are those who refuse to blindly acquiesce to the dogmas of the Roman Church, continuing to search and think for themselves.

No one in the world can pretend to know the truth. Least of all myself. Therefore, it is not up to me to contest in a dogmatic way the conclusions of the fathers of the Church, but to convey my personal experience, my vision of the world. Although I have never been baptized, I feel profoundly Christian. I believe I live in a Judeo-Christian culture. But it seems to me that, by definition, a predetermined doctrine does not allow for evolution and that only a confrontation of the various interpretations can favour an advance along the path of knowledge.

Although subjected to the screening of ecclesiastic censorship, the New Testament maintains traces of the doctrine of reincarnation. Let us reread the Gospel according to St Matthew, 17: 9–13,

As they were coming down from the mountain, Jesus cautioned them, saying: 'Tell no one about this vision, until the Son of Man has risen from the dead.' The disciples then asked him, saying: 'Why do the scribes say that Elias must come first?' He answered and said: 'Yes, Elias is indeed to come and he will restore all things, but I say unto you, Elias has already come and they did not know him, but they did to him whatever they wished. And the Son of God will suffer equally in their hands.' Then the disciples understood that he was speaking of John the Baptist.

Therefore, John the Baptist is presented as being the reincarnation of Elias. This is confirmed by Matthew, 11: 13–15,

For all the prophets and the Law have prophesied until John the Baptist. And he, if you will believe me, he is Elias who will return. He who has ears to hear, let him hear!

Jesus, when he was on the Mount of Olives, could not fall asleep, so he descended towards Jerusalem. There, he met Nicodemus. They talked for a long time and Nicodemus asked him (John 3: 4):

'How can a man be born and already be old? Can he enter into his mother's bosom and be born a second time?'

Christ's answer remains at the centre of infinite controversies on the part of the interpreters of the scriptures. The 'official' translation is the following (Bible of Jerusalem):

'To enter the kingdom of God, you will have to be born from above.'

But certain Hellenists state that it should read 'be born again', which would confirm that Christ professed the doctrine of reincarnation!

Reincarnation was, therefore, a subject which was not unknown to the early Christians, but there was a censorship of Christ's words on the subject. The great instigator of this was none other than Paul, the apostle of the Gentiles. Saul of Tarsus, baptized Paul, was the only one of the apostles not to have known Christ when he was alive. A fervent Pharisee, a mercenary paid by the Romans, he persecuted the Christians before his conversion. He then came into conflict with John, the heir to Christ's message. A great admirer of Roman power, Paul wanted to give the Christian Church an organization and a power based on the Caesarian model.

Today's Catholic Church, or rather, its hierarchical, dogmatic, commercial caricature we owe to Paul. That Church is the 'great whore' which St John's Apocalypse speaks of as the 'courtesan dressed in purple and scarlet'. It is an institutional church whose downfall is predicted in St John's Apocalypse (Chapter 17), for it has failed to respect the law of love dictated by Jesus of Nazareth:

> Come hither and I will show you the judgement of the great harlot, that sitteth upon many waters; with whom all the kings of the earth have surrendered to debauchery . . . A woman mounted on a scarlet beast, a beast with seven heads and ten horns . . . The seven heads are the seven hills on which the woman is seated . . . The woman you see is the giant city which reigns over the kings of the earth.

That giant city is Rome, with her seven hills and ten districts. The papal tiara bears three crowns, a sign of supremacy over kings and emperors. Rome will become the centre of the world once again, when the Antichrist makes it his capital after the death of the last pope, announced by the prophesy of St Malachi (author of the Book of Malachi in the Old Testament, c464–424 BC). And according to that prophesy Pope John-Paul II will be the one before the last.

If the Pauline Church sometimes outrages me, it is precisely because I feel deeply Christian and it is painful for me to see Christ thus betrayed, adulterated by an infantile iconography in which the infinite God becomes personalized, turned into a homely grandfather with a florid beard, in an attempt to lure the common man, to maintain him in a state of fear while enticing him with birds of paradise or threatening him with flames of hell.

To further his objectives, Paul rewrote the history of Christianity, creating his own version, suited to his ends. He started by omitting the fact that Jesus and his disciples were Jewish, an 'oversight' which laid the foundations for a latent anti-semitism in Europe, which would warrant the French extreme right-wing party's racist declarations and would culminate in the horror of Hitler's genocide. Jesus was not a simple carpenter, as we are told, but a Jewish aristocrat. The gospels by Luke and Matthew tell us that he was a direct descendant of King David. He is therefore the pretender to the throne of Israel, usurped by Herod and it is due to that title that he is received by the notables at Cana, for example. He entered Jerusalem by the Fishes' door – as predicted in the prophecy of Zechariah (9: 9),

> Rejoice greatly, O daughter of Zion!
> Shout for joy, O daughter of Jerusalem:
> Behold thy King comes to thee,
> He is victorious, He is triumphant
> Humble, riding upon an ass . . .

Jesus is a Messiah, the divine, the 'anointed One', the spiritual guide, the oracle, but he is also the king. Every sovereign of Israel was considered as a Messiah; the term was applied to David and his successors. They were 'anointed' kings by divine right, as were the kings of France, who were 'anointed' by the holy chrism in the basilica of Rheims.

As for Mary, she was a direct descendant of Solomon and the Queen of Sheba, which means she was a half-breed. Have you never wondered why, in a country where hospitality is a duty, a pregnant woman was refused shelter in a hostel and had to give birth in a stable? Nobody seems to have asked this question. There is a simple explanation for it: Mary had black blood in her veins. In fact, many representations of the Virgin are black: the du Puy Virgin, the Virgin of Chartres, Saragossa and those of Saintes-Maries-de-la-Mer are all black Virgins.

Besides, the Virgin was the first to be sacrificed by the essential falsification concerning the Trinity. The Christian, therefore Jewish Trinity, is directly inspired by the Egyptian Trinity which is made up as follows: the unique God, with an unpronounceable name, who when materialized becomes Osiris, God the Father; Isis, the black Virgin who gives birth to Horus; Horus the Redemptor, divine son of Father and Mother. Does that story sound familiar? It was, nevertheless, written 10,000 years before the advent of Christianity. But Paul, a visceral misogynist, for whom woman cannot be dissociated from sin, erased the feminine element from the Trinity. For, is it not astonishing to find in the Christian Trinity, the Father, the Son . . . and the Holy Ghost? Why conjure away the Mother in this fashion? Should we not see in that the source of an undeniable misogyny on the part of the Church?

I beg the reader's permission to present herewith my definition of the Trinity, such as it came to me during my meditations. Far from distancing myself from the subject, I am at the very heart of it. God created the world because he desired to do so. The whole, the one, the absolute, the river of infinite and eternal love is not conscious of its existence. To contemplate itself it must divide itself into two: God the Father, the one who contemplates, and the celestial Virgin, the one who allows herself to be contemplated – the *chaos* of the Greeks, the Maya of the Hindus. Through the active will of the Father, the celestial Virgin is going to create all the worlds, all existing things. That shock will engender the Son, the divine Word, the spark which will name and therefore animate each form created by the Mother.

But having wanted to contemplate itself, the absolute one loses its primordial unity. The whole becomes multiple, it disperses itself. Issued from divinity, made in the image of God, man is himself fragmented and limited by his prison of flesh. But if his body is linked to matter, his soul, a reflection and parcel of the great cosmic whole, aspires to renew the fusion with the one, to dissolve into divine light. But in order to attain that spiritualization, man has to go through different stages. His re-integration within the whole presupposes successive reincarnations.

If the Catholic Church rejects reincarnation, the doctrine itself has, nevertheless, many adepts. But the time has come to state exactly what one means by reincarnation. What are the mechanisms which govern the transmigration of souls? There again, it is not a question of imposing a system, but of stating a personal creed. Perhaps the sceptical reader would care to examine the following points; these may well answer some of the questions he asks himself. As for raising questions, reincarnation certainly does for the neophyte. From the most anecdotal – can one reincarnate as an animal – to the deepest – what is the meaning of our life on earth?

Since the original fall, man has become separate from divine light. He is the prisoner of matter, on what I would call the third energy level, that is to say the state of incarnation, of incorporation, which constitutes our present terrestrial condition. For between absolute light and brute matter, there is a series of intermediary stages, from the most dense to the most subtle, from the most inanimate to the most spiritual. Every being aspires to celestial life, but that transmutation towards spirituality is an extremely slow ascension. The soul progresses by stages, gradually detaching itself from matter.

On the first energy level, we find the lemurs and the humanoids who have just left the animal kingdom. Then come, on the second energy level, the cave dwellers characterized by their upright stance and the discovery of tools and fire. The third energy level is that of *Homo sapiens*, humans capable of abstraction, science and knowledge – contemporary man. When a human being dies he goes on to the fourth energy level, the Hades of the Greeks, a luminous, incorporeal world where the soul lives not outside time, but in a slowed down, prolonged temporality. It is this world which is described by the people who have come back from deep comas. In those famous near-death experiences, which occur during so-called 'clinical deaths', people see themselves travelling in a coloured world, in fascinating places where they meet other shadows.

But that fourth level is not the souls' ultimate destination. It is a kind of threshold, an obligatory passage. There the souls perfect themselves, become truer. For God being mercy, all faults are forgiven. To imagine a hell where the sinners are thrown into the flames or thrust into cisterns full of boiling oil is an insult to divine mercy! The vilest of sinners will be absolved, but it will be some time before he encounters divine light. In fact, on the fourth energy level the souls are in a kind of fog, still far away from the dazzling luminosity of the divine. Some will even be content to remain in that state: to aspire to divine light, one must have preserved a spark of that divinity in the depths of one's being.

But some will want to climb higher, towards God, nearer that total light, vaguely perceived as shining from above, which attracts them. The higher levels appear to them as having an extraordinary brilliance, like the steps of a crystal ladder. Therefore they desire to climb to heaven. When that desire for elevation invades us completely, the guardian of the threshold comes to us saying:

'You can stay here longer or else you can return to earth to try and improve yourself, to efface all the negative actions which are imprinted on your envelope.'

One chooses to return, in spite of the pain which the return into matter entails. There is, therefore, no one on earth who has not accepted the exact conditions of their incarnation,

family, body and all sorts of handicaps. Under no circumstances can a man be reincarnated as an animal. Although
some people would want to believe that a man who has lived
like a swine should come back to earth in the guise of a pig,
this is a misconception of divine law which rules that evolution must always progress towards higher levels. To return to
earth, we always choose a human form.

During that new life we will try and separate the wheat
from the chaff and purify ourselves. If we are successful, when
we die we will have access to a new level of wisdom and truth.
The fifth energy level corresponds to paradise. The sixth level
is that of hidden memories. There man rediscovers the
memory of all his past lives and can contemplate the journey
he has made towards God.

Finally, the soul reaches the seventh energy plane, coming
face-to-face with God, finding ecstasy in communing with the
whole. Thus, little by little, the soul ascends towards that
source of light of colossal brilliance, that headlight of goodness and of justice with which it wants to fuse and find ultimate happiness in the original unity once again. An exemplary
existence, an illumination, can bring us closer to the goal
more rapidly, but as a general rule the process is extremely
slow and can sometimes take millions of lives. The kingdom
of light is not that easily reached.

To elevate oneself, one has to first of all lighten one's soul
and deliver it from the dross left by negative actions committed in the course of our previous lives. For all negative actions,
all sins to use Christian terminology, have consequences in
our destiny. It is what the Hindus call *karma*, the law of cause
and effect. That can be summarized by a Biblical saying: one
always reaps what one has sown. To perform a bad action is
already to take a destructive path, for there is no word that
does not have an echo in eternity. If we do good deeds, we will
be able to progress towards the light. If we perform evil deeds,
we will have to mend our faults, in this life or in another one.

But this is not a punitive, revengeful law. Karma is not the law of retaliation: 'an eye for an eye, a tooth for a tooth'. It concerns the creation of harmony in our lives. The beginner who wants to learn to play a musical instrument will, at first, occasionally be out of tune, but he will learn by those mistakes what to avoid, how to place his fingers to attain the purity of absolute sound.

We always choose to reincarnate in a body which seems the most apt to help us correct errors from the past. Thus a dictator responsible for thousands of atrocities will come back in the body of a blind beggar-woman, condemned to suffer all the humiliations and all the suffering in the world. One who was an executioner will become a victim. These are, of course, extreme examples, but the mechanism is just as valid for a tyrannical tormentor as for a vilifying bigot.

I remember being a prostitute in the 18th century. It is the only life in which I can recall being a woman. During the reign of Louis XV, I was a child who was taken from her family for the pleasure of the king. I died at the age of seventeen after a short life of lechery spent on the Champs-Élysées, where the brothel frequented by the king and his courtiers was situated. Having often been a priest, endowed with a certain power over people's spirit, I was beginning to become hardened. My heart had become insensitive to the suffering of my fellow men. In order to elevate myself I had to know Mary Magdalene's fate. I had to suffer humiliation, degradation and public disgrace.

But again this was not divine punishment. Every being has to go through different stages, experience different trials, has to experience every kind of feeling, from pride to humility, from avarice to generosity. For what would be the merit of a man who was pious out of weakness, fear or lack of imagination? How could a man who has not known the power of doing evil deeds claim to attain divine enlightenment? The utmost purity and wisdom is not that of the zealot, but that of the being who has gone through all the stages, who has done evil but then refuted it. It is the reason why Christ has always gone to the sinners and not to the righteous or the paragons of virtue. The great saints have all been great sinners who had a revelation, they are all repentants. At a certain moment in their lives they thought to themselves: 'I have no right to do evil. For that is not where the secret of wisdom lies'.

The real sage is one who has known all human weaknesses and who has, little by little, elevated himself and become transformed into an enlightened being. He can then hope to attain the seventh energy level and at the height of the spiritual ladder become an *avatar*, an exceptional being who has accepted reincarnation to try and absorb the negative mass which has been enveloping the Earth. Sometimes those avatars reincarnate on earth to improve our condition. They then become like spiritual vortexes which come to earth to absorb the negativity around them. When Christ healed blind men or cripples he was in fact relieving those beings of their karma. One can even see in those miracles a resplendent symbol of Christ's message. He who died for men came to show the way to an elevation towards God by liberating men from their karma.

I can hear the sceptics' objections. If the law of karma imposes my destiny on me, if my present life is but a consequence of my previous actions, what freedom, what free will do I have left? Is this not to condemn a man to the strictest of determinisms? A determinism which would not be social or atavistic, but cosmic? The best way to answer these questions is perhaps to take the image of a card player to whom a number of cards is distributed. He has not chosen his game, but from then on he has the freedom to lay on the table the card of his choice, good or bad. He is free to win or lose the game, just as we are free to come closer to divine light or to move away from it. We can accept or refuse the gifts from heaven. We can exploit them or let them lie neglected. In other words, we have the ability of accelerating or slowing down our own evolution.

I believe that, in some way, all is written, meaning that when we reincarnate we are part of a divine plan. We have chosen our life, we have seen what 'could' happen to us. But we have also been given that divine gift which is free will: you can avoid such a thing, but this other one will befall you; you cannot avoid that, but you can do this . . . To convey what my conception of free will amounts to I will give an example. I have always compared life to a train going at full speed into a huge marshalling yard. All the tracks are laid down, but it can go left or right, it can change direction at any moment, going back on the 'right track' or losing itself in paths which have no exit.

Far from condemning man to a deterministic fate, the law of karma renders him responsible for his acts. We are the sole masters of our existence, just as we are masters of our actions and our thoughts. We always have a choice: to act or not to act. This is easier to explain when we tackle the condemnation of reincarnation by the church. By making the individual responsible, this doctrine liberates man, freeing him from the grasp of a clergy whose intention is to rule over souls. Being responsible for our salvation, we no longer have any need for terrestrial intermediaries to elevate us towards the whole.

Having said this, it is also true that free will is a poisoned gift or shall we say a trial for our pride. Thanks to that freedom, we can proudly boast, in fact, that we conduct our lives according to our will. But, when things start going wrong, we turn to heaven and beg for help! But the guides from heaven, whether they are the great guides or our guardian angel, that protective energy which looks after us, can only intervene if we abandon ourselves totally, if we relinquish our free will! To say 'I do as I wish, but if I drown you fish me out' is to have an infantile conception of the relationship with the divine. Just as inappropriate is the kind of prayer which goes: 'Oh Lord, please help me win the lottery'.

True prayer consists in putting oneself completely in God's hands. 'I give up my free will, do with me what Thy will, for whatever You do, I know it is done out of love.' Only then do our guides intervene, putting us back on the right path. But the majority of us refuse to submit and perform that simple act. Is it because we guess that the will of God would often not suit our purposes? That he would never agree with our twisted ways of obtaining riches, power and love. Sensing this, people often prefer to keep their free will. We do 'what we want', which is not always good, and thereby create a weighty karma for ourselves, whereas if we allow ourselves to be guided, we can accelerate our evolution. We can skip the obstacles in our path towards divine light, avoid wandering down roads which lead nowhere. Ultimately, the wisest attitude is to submit completely to God. The true sage is one who has total humility.

It is by abandoning his free will that man can alleviate his suffering. For the return of the soul into matter is synonymous with pain. In this body made of flesh, the soul will know the pangs of desire, envy, hunger, thirst and illness. Hell, for the soul, is being on earth. But the notion of reincarnation helps us to bear this earthly condition which may seem to us so unjust. For the trials of life, as painful as they may seem, offer us the possibility of coming closer to higher energy levels, therefore nearer to the light and to the truth. As the philosopher Simone Weil said 'the great strength of Christianity is that it proposes not a remedy for suffering, but a use for it '. Furthermore, the law of karma offers an explanation for this suffering, a means of lightening karma or, at least, of shortening the time of reparation which separates us from God.

From this point of view, death itself is no longer a tragedy. In certain civilizations, the families joyfully celebrate the departure of the deceased towards a better world. Death is, in fact, a rebirth, an elevation on the celestial ladder. As far as I am concerned, it has long since stopped being a frightening prospect. I know that my present life is my last. The iris has left the lower part of the eye.

3

The Tunic of Flesh

You gave me mud and I transformed it into gold
CHARLES BAUDELAIRE

To believe in reincarnation has become fashionable today. It is a joy to see that the last prejudices which hampered its diffusion are falling by the wayside in Europe. But with this acceptance comes the danger of a series of misinterpretations and dangerous deviations becoming widespread. It is undeniable that the transmigration of souls has a spectacular side to it which fascinates the public. What a sensation one can cause at a dinner party by announcing that in the past one was a maharani or a conqueror! Past existences are often used to flatter a dissatisfied ego or, for that matter, an inflated ego. For there can be some pride in stating what a miserable past life experience one had, as if to say 'Ah, if you knew how much I suffered!' The moralists have taught us to be very wary of such vanities.

Nowadays we see meditation centres and other such dubious places flourish on every street corner, promising 'guaranteed results' and the solution to every problem which the passer-by might have, thanks to so-called 'rebirth' or 'regression' methods. These might entail a reawakening of the memory of past lives, by certain more or less scientific techniques. A therapy which is meant to bring us paranormal powers or professional success in a few sessions! There is no stopping progress: yesterday psychoanalysis would explain people's neuroses by exploring the traumas of early childhood, now one rides a machine to travel back in time. These practices, sometimes applied by veritable charlatans who feed on other people's despair, can be a real danger.

In effect, the search for our past lives cannot take place without preparation. Such a quest cannot be undertaken due to simple curiosity: it presupposes that one is already sufficiently advanced in one's personal path. Just imagine for a moment what a tremendous psychological shock it would be for an individual to suddenly become aware that this life is but a link in a long chain of incarnations. Does he not risk losing his reason or simply 'switching off' from reality? If Isis' veil covers our eyes it is perhaps so that we should not be blinded.

Misunderstood, the belief in reincarnation leads to a regrettable detachment from reality. Confronted with the difficulties of daily existence, the temptation to take refuge in the past, in past lives, is considerable. In any case, it is evident that 'regression' means exactly that, to 'regress'. It is no longer a question of going forwards but of turning deliberately back, towards the past!

Furthermore, it could encourage a certain fatalism. 'All that happens to me is the consequence of my past lives, my personal dramas are the issue of yesterday's faults, therefore there is nothing that I could do to improve my fate.' If true life is elsewhere, why should I do today what could be done in a future life?

These misconceptions have led me to declare that in no way is a knowledge of past lives necessary. I would even go so far as to say that it is it quite anecdotal. How can the fact of knowing that I was a Mongol prince or a usurer in Lombardy help me in my present life? Will learning that I have asthma because I was asphyxiated with a feather pillow in the past help to cure me? To search for one's self in past lives is like looking for an almond in an empty shell. What a waste of time, when the time granted us is so short! If reincarnation and its inevitable consequences, karma, should have something to teach us, it is precisely the importance of our present life. It is here and now that man progresses and attains divine light. For if life on earth is but a spark compared to the eternity of higher energy levels, it is nonetheless an opportunity for evolution. It is by our daily behaviour that we can make our karma lighter.

This is the reason why the adepts of reincarnation lend primordial importance to our passage on earth. To retire from the world and become a recluse is not, in my view, the foremost path to wisdom. We should not run away from reality, but should endeavour to achieve whatever we have come to earth to achieve. To have faith in reincarnation should not mean taking refuge in the past, nor having a fatalistic attitude regarding the future: reincarnation is fundamentally an encouragement to act in the present.

To live in the present is, first of all, to accept the rules which govern social life. To be successful is not a crime, it is simply a reward for the efforts expended. There is no shame attached to earning money, on condition that one does not turn it into an end in itself. I have always had a curious relationship with money. I remember one day when, returning from the barracks, my father had thrown his jacket on the back of a chair. I took advantage of the situation and took his wallet. I then went down into the street and distributed the bank notes to passing strangers! My father caught me red-handed and administered a memorable thrashing with his military belt.

In spite of the poverty I experienced during my childhood, I felt a kind of contempt for that money which gave others all that I could not have. I never dreamt of the bicycle or the roller-skates which my mother could not give me. By the same token, even if I happened to admire the physical beauty of some of my companions, I would not have exchanged places with them for all the gold in the world. Changing my body would have meant changing my brain, my spirit, my imagination, my experiences. I felt that nature had bestowed upon me an intelligence, a vivacity of spirit which my companions did not necessarily have. I had fantastic gifts which largely compensated for the lack of fortune or of looks.

Today I earn a great deal of money, yet my attitude has in no way changed. I continue to distribute it widely, though not haphazardly, to try and help others. Money should never be an end in itself, but rather a means of acquiring a certain freedom of movement. I allow myself one luxury, space: I live in a large flat, painted white, in which there is practically no furniture, with the exception of some paintings and a vast library.

It is a well known fact that material comfort does not bring happiness. To be happy today is a difficult task for someone who refuses to wear blinkers, for we live in troubled times. The earth is being subjected to disturbing tensions. Pollution, poverty, famine, earthquakes, cyclones, epidemics, overpopulation, all those black clouds which darken our daily lives and endanger our future. A great number of our contemporaries opt for one of several escape routes either by taking all sorts of drugs or by joining one of those sects which one sees sprouting up everywhere. In either case there is self-destruction, be it physical or spiritual.

These menacing conditions and this generalized unease are due to the fact that we are actually in a transitional period. We are leaving the era of Pisces which started some 2,000 years ago with the coming of the Messiah, to enter into the era of Aquarius. Christ took great care to emphasize his association with Piscean times. Symbolically, the Bible tells us that he chose fishermen to be his first disciples, that he walked on the waters and threw his fishing nets. Once resurrected he ate fish

(Luke 24). The Greek word *ichtus* which means 'fish' is also an acronym which can be translated as 'Jesus Christ, Son of God, Saviour' (*Jesu Khristos Theou uios Sôter*). It was only later, in AD 325, that during the Council of Nicene the symbol of the fish was abandoned as symbolic of Christ and was substituted by the Latin cross.

The Christian era is the last phase of the age of steel, or Kali-Yuga. The era of Aquarius which succeeds it will be the era of gold. But the passage from one to the other will not be smooth. The transition period started in 1914 at the beginning of the 20th century 'when the erring Jew lay down his sack . . .' meaning the signature of the Balfour treaties in London which promised the Jews a home country in Israel. The sign of a cycle which has come to an end: banished from the Holy land, the scattered Jewish diaspora gathers together again to lay the foundation of the State of Israel.

And in the same way that in a theatre three knocks announce the curtain is going up, the new era of Aquarius is announced by three shocks: the First World War, the Second World War and the third shock . . . alas! It is imminent, even though it may be difficult, even dangerous, to give precise dates. Whatever its exact moment, this passage from one era to the next is already provoking a feeling of deep anguish which pervades us all in varying degrees. A malaise which the Roman Church is unable to pacify. But this is not surprising since it is, literally, no longer of our time. Deaf to warnings, apparently unconscious of the urgency of the situation, the Pauline Church busies itself with internal disputes arguing endlessly about liturgical questions. A now archaic institution, it seems incapable of answering our questions.

This failure of the church reinforces the disenchantment of the young, who, disoriented, don't know who to turn to or where to go. Taking refuge in politics is no longer a viable alternative. With the downfall of the Communist regime, the last bastion of our socio-political illusions has floundered. At the end of the 1940s and during the 1950s, all young people were Marxists, including me. I passionately believed that Marxist ideology was going to save the world! Luckily my first trip to the East opened my eyes. I realized that the egalitarian dictatorship was a crime against humanity. History has just provided us with the ultimate evidence, which must have convinced those who remained incredulous and still believed in the utopia of Communism.

Deprived of ideals, the young seek escape from an intolerable reality and throw themselves wholeheartedly into artificial paradises. What they find is the hell of dependency; they become the victims of pseudo-Oriental or pseudo-scientific sects which exploit their despair. Become a master in ten lessons! Awaken your inner energies by flash-meditation! Learn the techniques of rebirth! So many baits thrown by so many sharks. The prophets have warned us: 'Woe to the end of time, when sects will multiply and false gods arise!'

As a result of the moral bankruptcy of the political and religious institutions, a strong current of 'exoticism' is emerging. We go elsewhere, to other cultures and other religions, seeking the answers for our existential anguish. In my view, this is the wrong approach, for if we have chosen our particular body at the moment of incarnation, it is not by chance that we are born in a certain geographical place, and of a certain race, or culture. It is with those inherent qualities that we must work. If it was my destiny to retire into an ashram, I would probably have been born in India. But I was born here, in the West, in the Basque country, at a distance of 5km from the French border, with that incredibly rich Atlantean and Celtic inheritance. I live in a Judeo-Christian civilization and it is within Christianity that I must look for answers. It is not a question of asserting the superiority of Western culture over Oriental civilizations. Buddhism, Zen or Muslim Sufism are sublime philosophies, but I must cultivate my garden with the tools I have been given.

Unfortunately the Western world is going through a crisis of values. Without guidance or reference, the young, in particular, are easy prey for all kinds of impostors. When I was a child, I was constantly confronted with extraordinary heroes, people who knew the meaning of sacrifice. My father was executed by Franco because he refused to betray his Republican ideal. My mother fought all her life for her beliefs. Afterwards I found my role models in French heroes, such as the Blériot brothers (fathers of French aviation), Georges Guynemer (a French hero of the First World War): these were men whose aim was to overcome their limitations. But now these values of disinterested devotion no longer find an echo. Each person is enclosed in his own greedy egotism, isolated in his vehicle or in front of his TV set. We have gone back to the state of confusion and incomprehension which reigned in the tower of Babel. The radio and television channels multiply, people 'zap' away and all the speeches are mangled, languages criss-cross and politicians talk meaningless drivel. Babel is everywhere.

Nevertheless, it is in such difficult times that one must be doubly vigilant. One reads in the New Testament that one has to keep one's house in order, for God will come 'like a thief' when we least expect Him. Our house, meaning our conscience, but also our body, must be kept sane and purified. Alas, that purification was deemed impossible by the Fathers of the Church very early on. Throughout the centuries, our Judeo-Christian civilization made the body an anathema, considering it the source of all temptations and vices. A constant reminder of our fall, seat of those powerful forces which are our senses, it brings us nearer our animality when we would rather be angels. The Greeks had already conceived the notion that the body was the coffin of the soul, a prison made of flesh which nailed the spirit to the world of appearances preventing it from contemplating essential ideas. For the Manichaeans, as for censors within the Church, the flesh is in fact the indomitable beast, the seed of corruption which perverts the spirit. According to them, in order to attain salvation one must, first of all, despise everything that reminds us of our body. Thus, the glorification of asceticism, of virginity: hence self-flagellation. The monk who enters a monastery must leave his body behind at the entrance. The tunic of flesh can only divert his attention in his quest for truth.

Luckily, there have been a few humanists to remind us that a sane spirit cannot be dissociated from a healthy body. Is the body not God's creation, just as much as the soul? Consequently does it not merit our utmost consideration? More important still, is it not a parcel of the whole, a reflection of the cosmos which is the expression of God? Therefore, my body is as sacred as all the forms which have been created by the supreme energy. Hermes Trimegistus, Hermes Thrice Greatest, says in *The Emerald Table*: 'What is below is like what is above and what is above is like what is below'. There is a correspondence and a harmony between our microcosm and the universe's macrocosm. We human beings are ourselves a structured cosmos in which all the realms are contained – the mineral realm for example, for we are composed of metals and water and are, consequently, ruled by the moon. Like plants, we have a vital sap, the blood which runs in our veins. We are, therefore, subject to the sun just as the plants are. If we can know the world, it is, in some sense, because we are a synthesis of nature. In other words, our body is the means we have of experiencing, by analogy, divine power.

Although it may bring suffering, our body, that 'prison of flesh', is also the instrument by which we will re-conquer grace. In short the body is the safety net which caught us when we fell from grace and, by the same token, it will be the stepping-stone thanks to which we will gradually ascend, stage by stage, towards divine light. The flesh is, therefore, not completely negative. It is in fact the instrument of salvation, provided we put it to good use.

Contrary to what certain Manichaeisms may state, man is

not condemned to live split between these two conflicting elements, the body which would drag him down and the soul which would seek to elevate him. Man is a tertiary being, reuniting in himself body, spirit and soul. These three elements should complement each other. Our physical organs allow us, during our first apprenticeship after birth, to understand the physical world around us. That empirical awareness becomes, by association, thought. Through meditation we sharpen our senses and thereby expand the limits of our knowledge and reach the other side of reality.

Linking the physical body with that state of awareness, there are along the spinal column a series of energy centres which Hindu philosophy calls chakras, a Sanskrit word meaning 'wheel'. These are occult points linked by subtle channels where a double vital energy circulates; the double spiral is similar to the DNA's spiralling structure which contains all the genetic information. This energy is called kundalîni.

There are seven main chakras; they each have a function which corresponds to certain qualities. The first chakra, or base chakra, is situated on the perineum and rules the physical roots of our being. It rules, therefore, our first relationship with the world and is also the seat of the lowest, most primitive instincts. It is visualized in the colour red. The second chakra is situated in the groin, where our reproductive centre is situated. It is the seat of our sexual power and of our creativity. Its colour is orange. The third chakra is situated at the level of the diaphragm. It is the centre of our mental capacities. This is a double centre for it rules, simultaneously, the understanding of physical emotions and the birth of divine abstraction. Its colour is yellow. The fourth chakra is the heart, the seat of our feelings of love. It rules self-love, but also the love of others. It is visualized by the colour green. The fifth is the chakra of the throat, of the word, of communication and of judgement. Its colour is blue. The sixth chakra, situated in the centre of the forehead, is also called *ājna*, the third eye.

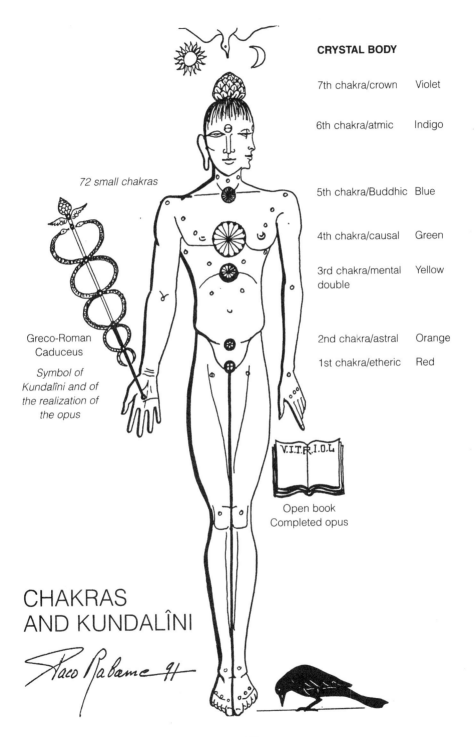

CRYSTAL BODY

7th chakra/crown — Violet

6th chakra/atmic — Indigo

5th chakra/Buddhic — Blue

4th chakra/causal — Green

3rd chakra/mental double — Yellow

2nd chakra/astral — Orange

1st chakra/etheric — Red

72 small chakras

Greco-Roman Caduceus

Symbol of Kundalîni and of the realization of the opus

V.I.T.R.I.O.L

Open book Completed opus

CHAKRAS AND KUNDALÎNI

67

The eye of truth, the horn of the unicorn, the seat of supra-sensitive knowledge, it represents the awakening of consciousness. Its colour is indigo. Finally, the seventh chakra is on the top of the head, between the fontanels. It is the lotus with the thousand petals – universal consciousness. It is through here that cosmic energy penetrates. Its colour is violet.

The Greeks symbolized the kundalîni energy, that vital force, by the Caduceus, Mercury's winged wand around which two serpents intertwine, and which doctors and pharmacists chose as their emblem. In other cultures the horse is the animal that symbolizes kundalîni. Lancelot, Percival and the Knights of the Round Table went on their quest for the Holy Grail on horseback. Their horse was white, representing the purity of the initiates' quest. The image of a higher spirituality is represented by the winged horse, such as Pegasus, mount of gods. At the summit of that hierarchy, one finds the unicorn, an emblem of the adept who has attained divine unity.

By awakening the upper chakras, man succeeds in heightening his body's capacities. He spiritualizes the body which manages to detach from physical matter and go into a subtler essence which opens it to knowledge. By meditating, notably by visualizing the colours of the chakras, man can act on his physical body, he can heal lesions, balance his passions and guide his aspirations towards God.

By orchestrating the kundalîni energies, playing them as one plays a musical instrument, man can put himself in harmony with the world. That was the message of the Pantheist religions: 'Keep your lyre attuned'. To be able to play that lyre, to make its strings vibrate fully, one has to know how to meditate. This does not mean to think about a given subject, but to create an inner void, an empty mental space, in order to immerse oneself totally in the present. No longer desire, no longer expect. We have to be in a state of absolute neutrality in order to become conscious of our self.

But that kind of meditation requires long practice. There are many blockages to overcome. Initially one is afraid of what might happen when thoughts no longer ponder on some subject and wander without limits, taking the spirit to unknown and dangerous pastures. Man is afraid that his murky shadow might produce inadmissible thoughts, lusty, sadistic or masochistic desires, awakening a mass of moral turpitude which lay sleeping within him. Fearing to open the door to his old demons, he prefers to direct his thoughts to precise subjects such as his work, his children, the wife he loves. But to stop there is to refuse to take the decisive step on the way to knowledge. The alchemist has always warned the apprentice: the research must begin with the *nigredo*, which is to say the descent into hell. We all have sadistic thoughts. Who has not dreamed of killing once in his life? To confront our negative desires, to hold them up to the light, is to accept oneself.

In a previous life, I was a priest during the Inquisition. I have tortured people. During my meditations, images of torture came back to me. I saw myself in dark cellars eagerly preparing the tongs and red-hot irons. It was in Toledo and I was close to the Grand Inquisitor Torquemada, a man of unrelenting cruelty whom I had to assist in his base deeds. Rather than rejecting those dark areas of my soul, I considered them objectively. I had the courage to exhume those terrible deeds and to exorcise them, not by savouring them but by examining their many facets. I descended into the muddy lowlands of my inner self and found blemishes which I inherited from my past lives, forbidden books I had read, wars I had fought, the horrors I intuitively felt in Auschwitz. But I managed to burst the abscess.

That is a stage on the path of truth which cannot be avoided. To look into the sewer of filth which simmers in the lowest parts of ourselves is essential. Didn't Oedipus have to kill his father and marry his mother to become conscious and know himself? 'Know thyself' – the great Socratic maxim – is the worthiest of human projects. But how many of us manage to achieve it? How many are content with a superficial self, fashioned by family or by society? For one must be careful, it is not a question of acquiring 'knowledge' about oneself, such as psychoanalysis can offer, which explains our lapses, our dreams, our neurotic behaviour. To really know one's self is to transform one's being, it is a long struggle which allows us to refine, to spiritualize our body of flesh, gain access to our essence, our subtle body. Then we reach the *albedo* which frees us from material bondage. A liberation which will finally allow the *rubedo* to take place, the reintegration into the divine whole.

To attain the mental void necessary for meditation, one has to master some simple techniques. I begin by taking a deep breath, from the lower stomach towards the upper part of the lungs, before expiring the carbon dioxide. Then I listen. Literally, I am all ears. My attention is not directed to outer noises, but to an inner vibration, a kind of reverberation that emanates from my body. I try not to think of anything. This waiting – which is never waiting for something – can take a long time, until my brain has quietened down completely and starts to participate in the waiting. Somehow I must subdue it.

Suddenly the void happens in me. I am invaded by an enormous force and a strong vibration resonates inside my body. The cosmic energies take hold of me and there is an explosion of joy in the absolute silence, a feeling of wonder, of a primordial simplicity. These vibrations are very intense and can be visualized in fantastic colours which correspond to the degree of concentration or spiritual state at that moment.

The position is not important. It is not necessary to unhinge our knee joints to sit in the lotus position. I am not Oriental and I don't have a yogi's suppleness. I am content to sit comfortably in an armchair, legs uncrossed and my spinal column straight, the head leaning forwards slightly, the eyes half-closed, hands on the knees with palms turned upwards.

When and where should one meditate? Anywhere and as soon as an opportunity arises. It's true our daily obligations do not leave us many leisurely moments and people constantly complain that 'they don't have a minute to themselves'. But that is because people don't make enough effort. One always has time to isolate oneself. I am up at dawn and I take about ten minutes to meditate. On my way to the office, if the taxi cab happens to be caught in traffic, instead of becoming irritable because I am going to be late, I thank heaven for the opportunity and sitting comfortably on the back seat, I close my eyes. The driver probably imagines that I am not quite awake. In fact I am meditating.

At the office, I take the time to meditate between appointments. On the whole, in spite of a very busy schedule, I manage four or five daily pauses. With some determination and organization, each of us should be able to do that. It is not a question of losing touch with reality, but rather of effecting a kind of inner readjustment. It is not necessary to join a prayer group or ask some guru for advice. One has to become a 'prayer' oneself, by deep meditation, wherever one may be. I have often done that when travelling on the tube. If I have about 15 stations ahead of me, I know that I have time to concentrate. I invoke Isis the initiator, the black Virgin, the chthonic Virgin. Instead of feeling impatient or noticing my co-travellers' bad tempers, I create a void in myself. Eyes half-closed, I smile . . . without provocation. One must not generate aggression in people. If you mind your own business, stay in your corner, smiling, people leave you alone and end up by not even noticing you're there. I usually protect myself mentally by a simple act of magic, creating around myself a luminous boundary. I imagine myself enclosed in an egg with mirrors on the outer shell, whereas inside a soft light reigns, the famous golden pink light of the true Rosicrucians. On the outside, I am a mirror in which people see themselves reflected. When they look at me, it is their own image which I reflect. I am there physically, but invisible. All external aggression is dissipated.

It is thanks to these meditations and by totally immersing oneself in the present that one can master time. It ceases to exist or takes on the value which one decides it has. In my professional life, this is an essential tool. My business is fashion, of course, but I also deal in musical and cinema productions. I sometimes accumulate ten appointments in one day and in spite of that, I 'take my time'. I get up at 5.30 in the morning and I arrive at my office at 7.00. At that hour, there is nobody there, neither secretaries nor workers. This gives me the opportunity to do a few drawings, to plan my day. As for my appointments, I am always extremely punctual. The person who comes to see me has my total attention. I am totally open with him, without restrictions. My visitor of the moment has total priority over other concerns. He is there in the present moment and I am totally there for him, entirely open. There are no tricks or evasions, which means that we go straight to the subject. When somebody comes into my office, I ask: 'What brings you here? What can I do for you?'. This sets a lucid tone and the interview is rapid and concise, leaving one available for other things, once the matter at hand is dealt with.

'Keep your lyre attuned' simply means keep your body healthy and lead a sane and well-balanced life. I have always loved sports passionately. Physical effort gives me great pleasure and I find that it brings a feeling of serenity and peace. Exercise and its gestures bring harmony. Sport is also for me a way of relating to others, of developing a certain feeling of fraternity.

Care of the body does not necessarily mean cult of the body. For some ten years now, I have seen people dedicating themselves to body-building, adopting a Spartan discipline to develop sculptural muscles. Why not, one could ask, if it allows them to find a certain balance? But there is the great risk of missing the point. For such body-building means loving the body for itself, when we should love it because it is our main link with that 'other side', beyond matter.

We must not only take care of our bodies, we have to protect them against the ever-growing environmental hazards. For example, it is now almost impossible for me to go into a nightclub. The deafening music disturbs me terribly: my breathing becomes irregular, my eardrums buzz for several days afterwards, victims of an imbalance of the inner vibration which puts me out of touch with the world's harmony. These hazards are rampant in professional life too, making us neglect areas such as our eyes and our back. Completely ignored, the body is continually threatened by over-exertion. How can one expect to have a good mental balance if the physical roots are so unstable?

To love your body is, first of all, to have the courage to accept yourself as you are. That is the absolutely essential condition for any spiritual development to take place. We can quote Hermes Trimegistus once more, in *Corpus Hermeticum*: 'If you hate your body, my child, you cannot love yourself'. The Orientals and the Gnostics tell us exactly the same thing, inviting us to love our body as a Grail, a receptacle created by the will of God and in His image. It is through this tunic of flesh that we will understand the world and it is through it that we will understand our place in the cosmos. Therefore, the first gesture should be to look at yourself in the mirror. To accept yourself is not always easy if you do not correspond to the standards established by the fashion magazines. You should contemplate yourself and say: 'God gave me this appearance, I love it because He has. God is present in me'.

All progress in the quest of the inner Grail goes through the discovery and love of one's body. Let us remember that we chose it in order to lighten our karma. We have accepted that blemish which makes us ugly, that illness which overwhelms us, so that we may be elevated by humility or suffering. It is not a question of resignation or refusal of all the various therapies, but of learning to surpass one's limitation by exploiting whatever dispositions are innate or given. Therefore, the blind man will compensate for his lack of sight by developing his sense of hearing or of touch. Our body is full of potential qualities. Why are we waiting to discover them?

Some people, on the other hand, seem to make a point of destroying those possibilities by abusing their body with excessive smoking, drugs or other dangerous chemicals. Our breathing and our heart-beat are in the image of the movement of the ebb and flow which animates the earth, in the image of those phases of expansion and contraction which astronomers observe in the cosmos. Our lungs allow us to feel our oneness with the cosmos. The yoga masters know this, which is why they believe that the control of our breathing is the first step in meditation. Cigarettes have always seemed an aberration to me. Why persist in obstructing our link with God by polluting it with a layer of nicotine?

For similar reasons I do not eat meat. It is said in Genesis that on the fifth day God created the fish and the birds. On the sixth day he created animals and man. The animals, therefore, belong to the same 'generation' as man. An ox which is being taken to the slaughter-house knows he is going to die and this presentiment produces a terrible stress, a negative energy which the consumer of red meat will then ingest and this will disturb his body's energy centres. When the chakras are awake, eating meat provokes terrible burns all along the body's energy channels. It is like a red-hot iron at the base of the neck and on the solar plexus. Having said this, each person is free to choose. If you do not wish to evolve spiritually, you can eat as much meat as you wish, inject poison in your veins, destroy your chakras, deaden that fragile instrument which allows us to correspond with the world and the beyond. You will slow down the lightening of your karma.

On the other hand, fish and birds belong to a different realm and are adequate nourishment. One can also choose a strictly vegetarian diet, but it has become more difficult, sometimes even dangerous nowadays, as many vegetables are treated with chemicals or radiation and, consequently, do not have the same nutritional value as before. Even the organic vegetables are not all they seem! What a fraud some of these organically grown foods are! Many of the vegetables, fruits and cereals are contaminated by chemical fertilizers. The so-called 'normal' fields are side by side with organic ones: it is obvious that they are both subject to the same atmospheric pollution. Organic produce is a fake. Everything is poisoned. Acid rains spread violent poisons on our forests which slowly die of generalized cancer and, as for the radioactive cloud from Chernobyl, it didn't stop politely at your country's border. All the radiation that issued from the fusion of that uranium core has fallen on the earth, on the vegetation and on the rivers.

When we register these facts, we realize that taking care of our body means, necessarily, protecting our environment. How could it be otherwise, if we are all sons and daughters of the earth? In spite of all our efforts to lighten our personal karma, we are victims, albeit indirectly, of Gaia's deterioration. When will we understand that our fate is inseparable from that of our nurturing Mother? At the end of this millennium, a conjunction of negative energies threaten to drag the earth down into a destructive vortex.

This earth which supports us is, nevertheless, the most condensed form of divine love, it is the Holy Ghost for the Catholics, Maya for the Hindus, Gaia for the Greeks. She gave birth to us, she is an extension of our bodies: 'You were born of dust and to dust you will return'. Issued from the earth, born of her entrails, it is our duty to respect and protect her. For we have inherited one of the most beautiful planets of the galaxy, the blue planet. Blue like the Virgin's cloak, blue the colour of compassion. This heritage one must render fruitful and not condemn it to sterility, although, in the space of 50 years we have made a rubbish tip of it! We have been careless and irresponsible!

When I was a child, I remember one could fish for shrimps in every river in France. Now, most of them are transformed into sewers. When I arrived in Paris, I could still bathe in the Seine and drink its water without being afraid of catching all kinds of illnesses. Today . . .

What about the trees? What have we done to the trees? The tree is the loving impulse from the vegetable world toward the divine. Through its roots which dig deep down into the earth and by its crown which towers in the air, it unites heaven and earth. The tree is the earth's impulse towards its god, the sun, opening to him and generously producing oxygen for human beings to breathe. How do we thank the trees? By cutting them down, burning them and poisoning them; by depositing all kinds of garbage at their feet. Free a tree of the detritus which litters the ground and you will hear its branches rustle with pleasure. For those trees are alive, they talk! But we must know how to listen.

The last 25 years have been particularly destructive for the whole of nature. In one generation, we have destroyed our ecosystem. Held together by a fragile balance, the slightest disequilibrium can have dramatic consequences. We are just beginning to realize that our natural resources are not un-limited, that the oxygen layer which surrounds the planet and the layer of ploughable land are both very thin and both are now very damaged. Naturally, Gaia rebels. For some time now, not a year has gone by without there being an earth-quake somewhere in the world. Our planet suffers, moans, cries for help and we don't hear! The future of the earth is threatened. Materialists, ecologists and spiritualists all agree on this point.

Let us be careful not to mortally wound the generous Gaia. It is she who nurtures our needs. If she takes revenge, she who is pure will acquire a karma and this will not only block the passage of the planet to the higher energy level of Aquarius (of which we will speak again later), but in the coming years this will weigh on all of us, for we are all responsible.

Our earthly existence is, when all is said and done, about respect which is not synonymous with boredom or austerity. Respect for money because of the freedom it affords us, but not the cult of money. Respect for one's body without falling into narcissism. Respect for the earth, enjoyment of it and not inconsiderate exploitation of its riches. Respect for one of the most precious gifts we have been given, but without deviation: I am talking of sexuality.

All the traditions have invested sex with a sacred value. In the oldest religion, the Egyptian one, it is said that Seth, the brother of Osiris, jealous of the love that Osiris had for Isis, set up a trap for him and assassinated his brother cutting him up in pieces which he threw in the Nile. Desperate, Isis went looking for her spouse. She managed to find all the pieces, with the exception of his phallus, which a fish had swallowed. Deprived of his phallus, man is but a lifeless corpse. In ancient Greece, the temples housed statues of Priapus, the ithyphallic God, represented with his sex erect, symbol of fecundity and of life's continuity. One finds these images in Egypt and in Turkey, where the phallus is considered as the receptor of divine energy.

Alchemical studies distinguish between the three upper chakras and the three lower ones, which are linked to the material world and awake in the majority of people. In fact the third chakra is double: it combines the lower mental which corresponds to sexuality and the higher mental which corresponds to spirituality. This means that at the level of the diaphragm, man is cut in two. Sex is the link, the passage between man's procreative power and cognitive power. It is, therefore, the source of knowledge. But this knowledge had to remain secret in the past. Alchemists swore not to speak of sexuality, a law which was tacitly understood and accepted by all and which should not be broken, under any circumstances. Yet today everything is unveiled, exhibited. 'Woe to the time when the pearls fall into the river' – today, pearls of wisdom are thrown to the swine.

A great number of esoteric schools thought that they would gain access to spirituality via physical love. It is the 'humid way' which the alchemist speaks about or Hindu Tantrism. When a couple makes love, it becomes androgynous. The joined bodies become one and come nearer to divine whole-ness. The sexual union is the reflection of divine hierogamy which engendered the world. By using very special concentra-tion techniques, aimed at keeping alight the sacred fire, the adepts of that initiation path attain fantastic moments of exaltation.

But Tantric philosophy is a way full of traps for us Westerners, for we are unprepared for it. In India, children are massaged from a tender age to help them perceive their physical identity. They are not ashamed of their body, they know its resources, its energy. But we who bathe in Judeo-Christianity, we punish the body, we are castrators who encar-cerate the body in sewn garments, in corsets and collars. Constrained by taboos, the Judeo-Christian can only be a man subject to sexual prohibitions and inquisition. The number of victims of the Inquisition is estimated to have been around 50,000 people burned every month in Europe. The violence of that formidable repression is explained in part by the sexual frustration caused by the way in which the Catholics lived at that time. Cruelty and sadism became compensations for that ignorance of sacred sexuality. Unlike the Hindus, we had not understood that spiritual perfection comes from an existential fulfilment. One does not find God by cutting oneself off from the world, but in the love of another human being, a love that can include the pleasure of physical love.

The swing of the historical pendulum has always thrown man from one extreme to the other. After the repression generated by the Inquisition and after Anglican Puritanism, we have fallen into unbridled sexuality, the candid initiators of which were the hippies, who proclaimed total liberation from moral restrictions and the abolition of sexual taboos. They no longer hid their bodies and made love in groups. But freedom degenerated into dissipation, especially in the American homosexual community. Twenty years ago, people made love 20 times a day! In the 'blackrooms' people made love to strangers.

In 1980, Pluto, the planet of death, entered the sign of Scorpio, the sign of sexuality. At the same time, Aids was born. We had forgotten that the sexual act is above all a sacred act and that love also means respecting one's partner. Love is not a game! It is the meeting with another and one's elevation through him or her. At the moment of orgasm, one touches a spark of eternity. In popular language, always so expressive, one says 'to reach seventh heaven'. The physical act of love is also an expression of spirituality.

A terrifying illness, Aids, brought back some restraint to sexual practices. In 1995 Pluto left Scorpio, which predicts the discovery of a vaccination. But thousands, millions of victims had to die, before we said finally: 'That's enough'. Already the 'depraved' have been reduced to dust as in Sodom and Gomorrah (Genesis 18–19). We have returned to those dangerous times. Those versed in esoteric knowledge know full well that a danger much more terrible than Aids threatens humanity, if human beings do not mend their ways. By noting the consequences of great sexual promiscuity, one cannot help thinking that it was not by chance that the alchemists imposed secrecy on the subject.

On the portal of Notre-Dame, one can see on the central pillar the figure of the alchemist. He is lying down, asleep, and from his sex emerges a winged dragon. Higher, one can see the accomplished, sanctified alchemist, holding in his hand the book of knowledge, and plunging a staff in the dragon's mouth. St Michael thus terrified the dragon, the Bible's old serpent and in the same way, Theseus, following Ariadne's thread, finds his way out of the labyrinth and has to confront the Minotaur, a creature which is half human, half bull. St Michael symbolizes the man who wants to go back to his blessed angelic condition and who, in order to accomplish this, must confront his regressive tendencies. The winged monster is our imagination. With its sexual, erotic fantasies, it has the daemonic wings of the bat, a caricature of the angel of purity. It is the reverse of the mirror which we must, nevertheless, explore before gaining access to the truth.

But the reader will understand if I say no more, for there are paths on which the only possible guide is oneself. I cannot facilitate what must be a strictly personal quest. Everything has been written, everything can be read, be it in the Gnosis, in legends, in sacred architecture. One must make the effort to look, to read what the artist, the initiate has inscribed on stone or transmitted in parables. For knowledge of oneself is not transmissible. It is the end of a long personal labour, the quest of an entire life. St Luke tells us: 'Look and you will find' (Luke 11: 9).

4

The Whims of Fashion: Never Innocent

It is our spirit that we dress, not our body
YVONNE DESLANDRES

To live in the present means, among other things, to notice the changes in the world, the way things evolve from year to year, subtly revealing the values of that particular time. What phenomenon could be more typical of those metamorphoses than the world of fashion?

This explains the apparent paradox in my life. People often ask me how my quest for the eternal self, for the primordial centre, can be reconciled with working in the world of fashion, which means dealing with the most ephemeral, the most transient of things; the clothes we wear. From my point of view, this is not a contradiction. To understand the fluctuations of fashion one must understand people and their relationships with the world. Clothes are, in fact, extremely revealing. Being and seeming are not contradictory notions; they are closely linked and maintain an active dialogue, playing at mirroring each other incessantly.

In 1951, I entered the Beaux Arts partly by chance. Like every 17-year-old, I did not really know what path to choose. I was a gifted draftsman and thought I might become a painter. But a friend from my home district, Sables d'Olonne, was employed in the workshop of Auguste Perret (the inventor of reinforced concrete), and he convinced me that I should apply to study there.

'Why don't you try?' he asked. 'You will see, architecture is fascinating, you will like it.'

I followed his advice. I went to Paris and registered with the Beaux Arts National School for Advanced Studies, to study in Auguste Perret's workshop which had an excellent reputation. That was a tough school: mainly because freshmen had to go through a series of trials which often came very near to sadism. This went on during the whole of the first year.

In the early 1950s, this ritual was exacerbated by the fact that some of our elders had known the German prison camps and, in a way, they took their revenge on the novices for the maltreatment they had suffered. At the beginning of the year there were 500 pupils, at the end, the number of pupils had dwindled to approximately 30! These rituals had the advantage of reinforcing solidarity among the students. We all came from very different social backgrounds and we were all subjected to those somewhat violent tricks. The only way to bear this was to close ranks. It was almost a condition for survival. But the Beaux Arts school had advantages. We were tutored by mentors such as Auguste Perret or Hervé Albert, who built the cathedral of Algiers. These masters were great humanists and were always telling us that to be a good architect one had to play two parts in the world, meaning we had to excel as professionals and as men of the world, this world. They insisted that we should have an in-depth knowledge of our century, encouraged us to visit as many exhibitions as possible to learn about arts such as painting, sculpture and photography. We were also told to pay frequent visits to the cinema, the theatre and meet the people who were the foremost personalities in their chosen field, be it artistic or intellectual. To encourage this, they invited to the workshop the great spirits of the time, such as Zamansky, the eminent mathematician, or famous painters like Manessier, Carzou and Estève, and musicians such as Xenakis. All the 'intelligentsia' of the 1950s came and lectured on their concept of art which forced us to reflect on the problems raised by creativity.

Throughout those years I acquired a substantial general culture and opened myself to the world around me. The subjects taught at the Beaux Arts included art history of past civilizations. No creative person can pretend to be an innovator if he does not have a deep knowledge of ancient iconography. How can one measure one's personal contribution, if one ignores what has gone before? It may happen that we are perpetrating or imitating a tradition unknowingly, whereas the creative person, possessing general culture, can clearly identify his originality, without being deluded as to the source of his inspiration.

This education with its solid and concrete teachings was to be very useful to me in the future. Furthermore, I met some extraordinary people at the Beaux Arts, who were already very advanced in their esoteric research and who guided my steps. I discovered the books written by Fulcanelli which opened the world of sacred architecture to me, such as the Romanesque and Gothic abbeys, which hold the secrets of the brotherhood of the initiates. The cathedrals are not simple constructions built for the glory of God, but a synthesis, a revelation allowing us to penetrate the thoughts of our ancestors. Behind the visible stone lies an immense artistry, an ancestral knowledge which was perpetuated thanks to the initiates and to architects such as Viollet-le-Duc. The historical reconstructions he effected were not false, on the contrary, they were based on the esoteric tradition, a knowledge which allowed him to preserve the sacred message contained in the monuments he restored.

Hence, I developed what I call 'double sight'. This initially sees the form of the object, then takes an interest in its meaning. What is the message it carries? What does it really want to convey? What does it express? Little by little one progresses in one's research, with abiding curiosity, looking at the world in its nakedness, to draw out its magic. For if the object is presence, it is also revelation, being impregnated by divine mystery. Unfortunately, most people stop short at appearances, they do not make the effort of going further, of looking for the relationships which animate things and the fascinating connections between them. That 'double sight' I would also apply to fashion, in order to understand the symbolic and social role that clothes play in our lives. For the whims of fashion are not as innocent as they may seem.

By renouncing architecture to dedicate myself to fashion, I was not going into an unknown world. My mother had been first seamstress in Balenciaga's couture house in Spain, before becoming politically militant. At first, in order to pay for my studies, I put my craft skills to good use by making maquettes in the Beaux Arts workshops. From there I went on to do fashion maquettes. I designed handbags, belts and jewellery which I made myself and then offered to fashion designers. This is how I first met Balenciaga, Givenchy, Jacques Griffe, Saint-Laurent and Christian Dior. I sold them my drawings – I had a good pencil style. I also made buttons in the most unusual materials: I glued bits of vermicelli pasta or coffee beans on small Rhodoid plaques which I painted. The fashion then was Baroque buttons and the ones I made used to sell like hot cakes! Thanks to these small artefacts, I managed to subsist comfortably while putting one foot into the world of high fashion.

I quickly perceived that Parisian fashion designers were content to have what I considered to be a taste for the past. People complimented them by saying that their work was 'deliciously 1930s' or that they brought the belle époque back to life. My training had been the very opposite of this: we had concentrated on understanding and studying the contemporary world. Hence, I was horrified with this nostalgic trend. How could one do 1930s fashion in the 1960s? The world was in a state of flux and fashion was sinking into barren stagnation. This was an anachronism which I rebelled against with all the energy of youth.

That is when I began to feel I would like to present my own haute couture collection; when the seed was sown. I imagined a Dadaist collection, in a gesture of provocation and rebellion, in the hope of shaking off the inertia and hopefully promoting contemporary ideas. The teaching at the Beaux Arts had taught me that in all the great historical movements, there is a harmonious relationship between the different art forms. During the Baroque period for example, one can see correspondence between Borromini's architecture and Bernini's sculpture, Tintoretto's painting, the poetry by Jean de Sponde (a French poet and humanist, 1557–95) or Agrippa Aubigné (a French writer, 1552–1630). All these art forms show a taste for illusion, for curvilinear forms, for the ephemeral and ostentatious. These characteristics can all be found in the garments worn at the French court of the time. One could equally establish analogies between the functional architecture of the Bauhaus, abstract art at the beginning of the 20th century and the straight dresses of the 1920s.

The 1960s were the theatre of a fantastic revolution in the arts. New methods of expression were being discovered, like Optical Art or Kinetic Art. In every field novel techniques were being explored with one common characteristic – traditional materials were abandoned. Architecture was renouncing stone, sculpture was no longer using marble, painting put canvas aside. Martial Raysse and the Nice School were making pictures with neon, Sotto with steel wires, Julio Le

Parc worked on metal plaques and Quassar created inflatable furniture in transparent plastic. Music was no longer harmonic, but serial, dodecaphonic and electronic. Classical instruments gave way to inventions such as glass organs, ancestors of today's synthesizers, which were created by the Baschet brothers.

Fascinated, I was carried away by this formidable movement and decided to apply to fashion, a minor art, the gestures of these creative artists whom I admired. I too, was going to be innovative. I would abandon cloth, invented by the Egyptians 15,000 years ago, and substitute it with the latest contemporary materials. That is how I became interested in plastic, Rhodoid and aluminium, which had never been used in fashion before. I put needle and scissors aside and took up pliers and blowpipe. I soon put together some 'experimental' models. When I set myself this task it did not cross my mind that the result would be in any way futuristic. I was simply a little ahead of those who were behind their time.

At the end of 1964, I presented to the public 'twelve experimental and unwearable dresses made of contemporary materials'. These caused a great scandal. One has to remember the atmosphere in which fashion shows took place at the time: a lady barked the names of models, a veritable litany – up to 300 – and they all had grotesque names like 'The toad who died of love' or 'Night butterfly'. I found this amazingly silly and often very boring.

One can imagine the shock of a public used to that kind of fashion event when confronted with warrior girls, covered in metal armour made of aluminium triangles linked with rings or rivets, moulded in sheets of sliced Rhodoid. It was a revolution in high fashion, all the more so because it was the first time that black models had been used, all dancing frenetically to the sound of Pierre Boulez's 'Le Marteau Sans Maître'. Chaos and confusion broke out, an incredible tumult reigned, some people got up, screaming, horrified at the sight of these amazons dressed in chain-mail, swinging their hips to 'savage' music. Others manifested their approval in uproarious fashion under the perplexed eye of members of the Parisian bourgeoisie. The prank had worked.

Far from being discouraged by this scandal, I found it stimulating. I decided to continue along that line, all the more so because I had made a name for myself and orders were coming in from all over the world. That is how I left architecture, simply by wanting to put fashion in step with the 1960s' revolution! I didn't really feel that I was going back on ten years of study. Le Corbusier, whom I admired, used to say: 'Architecture includes the door knob'. By going into fashion, I was still working with man's environment. I also felt that it would give me the opportunity to give free reign to my imagination. The rules which govern architecture seemed very constraining to me. But I would later discover that fashion is far from being the gratuitous game I imagined it was at that time. It obeys rules which, though less well defined, are nonetheless inescapable.

As I progressed in my new profession, I began to ask myself certain questions. Why did fashion exist? What needs did it answer? What were the functions of a collar, a tie or other accessories? A complex phenomenon, a multi-faceted symbol, fashion can be seen from many different angles. What first comes to mind is that man conceived his first garment to protect himself from the elements. In my opinion this is a hasty conclusion. I will give you an example. When European explorers first set foot in Patagonia, on the southern-most point of South America, they discovered that the natives lived naked at temperatures of -15°C and wore only some amulets.

The first garment was, therefore, magical. It was an ornament, a fetish destined to attract the favour of powerful divine forces, such as lightning, fire, water and wild animals. By the same token, in the Amazon forest men and women put wooden plaques on their lips in order to resemble the sacred bird, to mimic totemic animals. In order to come closer to those divinities, they sacrifice a part of their flesh.

Cloth, invented by the Egyptians thousands of years ago, was a symbol of the Trinity. The thread, the one in the image of God, divides itself into two, the one who contemplates and the one who allows herself to be contemplated. The thread which links and the thread which weaves. Both mingle to create a world, the world of fabric. Represented in hiero-glyphic writing by a plaited half-basket which the Egyptians named *neth*, cloth was initially reserved for statues of deities and for the pharaoh, the living God. It had, therefore, an emi-nently sacred value. But all human creation becomes pervert-ed: leaving the divine shoulders, the garment descended to the royal court and from there to the middle-classes and then to the people. Having lost its sacred quality, it could only become a social emblem.

This deviation of the fundamental meaning of clothes was exploited in an exemplary fashion by Louis XIV who preferred to see his nobles ruin themselves acquiring lace and precious cloths rather than in feuds and internal strife. The following centuries inherited this idea of equating dress with a certain social rank. Each class was characterized by a particular type of costume. The clergy by the cassock, the judge by robes, nobility by the sword, the soldier by the uniform. The costume was a way of signalling which group one belonged to or the function one occupied in society.

Under these conditions, one can imagine that dress, an emblem of one's social position, would soon change into a sign of obedience, a social code. The tie is perhaps the most striking example; a noose to stifle all protests, a lead with which cattle are taken to work or to the slaughter-house, a self-inflicted slave necklace which the devotee of the golden calf wears. The tie is the rope around the neck of the bour-geois from Calais.

Nowadays, in our theoretically egalitarian times, the way people dress tends towards a functional uniformity. The priest abandons his cassock to mingle with the masses, distancing himself from the symbolic role which his costume represented. One can see that kind of evolution in the gradual abandonment of the use of hats, symbols of authority and affirmations of superiority. The height of this 'uniformization' of people was no doubt when Maoist China imposed the blue two-piece suit on the whole population. Under the guise of egalitarianism, this measure was part of a vast programme in which sexual impulses were to be channelled towards work. This would 'kill two birds with one stone' – control the demographic explosion and increase productivity! Far from being liberating, the rejection of the class garment in favour of an egalitarian monotony was but an extreme form of massive military enrolment.

The first attempt at destroying this system of functional uniformity was the hippy movement in the 1970s, the flower people who threw away their suits and ties and replaced them with flowered shirts and jewellery. Men and women wore the same wide tunics, the same painted jeans, personalized, and the same long hair. They created the first 'festive clothes', androgyne, announcing the new era of Aquarius. For dress is often used as a tool for sexual differentiation, or at least it has become that. The Greeks wore unisex tunics, the 'chiton', so that the sexes would not appear different except in certain circumstances where women differentiated themselves by their hairstyle and jewels. In Europe, up until the Middle Ages, the time of the courts of love and chivalry, the doublet was identical for almost everyone.

In France, the introduction of restrictive clothing for women was due to King Francis I. Although history tells us he was a great lover of women, he must have nurtured a secret aversion for them. Whereas before his reign the ladies of the

French court wore dresses as light and as supple as a second skin, he invented devices which would compress and oppress women socially. To keep women 'toeing the line', he imposed buskins on them, perching them on wooden platforms which were 10cm high which made their walk dainty but fragile. From then on, women had their waist cinched by a far-thingale, ancestor of the corset, and the movement of their heads limited by the famous weighty ruffed collars which held their necks. This sexist slavery was the invention of Francis I. He prevented women from living by impairing their movements and, therefore, curtailing their emancipation. If he loved them, it was only if they were domesticated: as tame objects. Deep down they must have terrified him. This subjugation became more and more refined in the following centuries.

It was only during the 20th century that this strait-jacket was thrown away and women, for their happiness or for their sins, went into active life. They adopted masculine trousers, thus expressing their desire to be treated as equals. We witness today a certain uniformity in the clothes for both sexes, at least during working hours. But at night women rediscover their femininity, become butterflies, attractive and flamboyant. This is a tendency which will become accentuated as we enter the era of Aquarius, at the dawn of the third millennium. As human beings will be exceedingly numerous, the hours of work for each person will be reduced and leisure activities encouraged. We will work only a few hours a day and then take off our working clothes, exchanging them for more comfortable, and colourful clothes. Man and woman will rediscover their creativity, become joyous.

From my point of view, unisex trousers are not a victory, nor a symbol of freedom. I see them rather as a constraint and an imposed discipline. An emblem of the Western world, it is not adopted by the rest of the world where the comfort of the djellaba and kaftan are preferred. When I go home, I put on a

Japanese kimono, a habit acquired when I first visited the land of the rising sun. It is true that fashion reflects social values, moral evolution and changes in people's mentalities. The adoption of trousers by Western women is a good example of that. When one evokes a civilization, the image that comes to mind is a type of dress, even before the architecture or political system of that part of the world. A period in history is marked, above all, by a way of dressing. This goes to show that fashion is not such a superficial social phenomenon as one might think.

The clothes we wear are like an envelope, symbolic of a particular time, permitting gestures which are characteristic of that moment in history. Each change in behaviour corresponds to an evolution in the dress of that particular time. The last radical break we have known occurred at the outbreak of the First World War. Until 1914 women were, in the majority, housewives, not only prisoners of social taboos but also enslaved by corsets, laced shoes and at times veils. Then, suddenly, the men were gone to the Front, to fight in the trenches, while, back home, women had to go out to work in the men's places, in the fields, in the factories, driving buses and trains. Woman herself cut the corset's strings, for it was so tight she could not bend down. She put her long dress away in the cupboard and substituted for it a pair of trousers or a short dress.

For different life styles, different clothes. Paul Poiret, the French fashion designer and decorator, helped by famous painters such as Vlaminck or Dufy, was content to adorn these lines which women had established for themselves between 1914 and 1918. For it is always the woman and not the designer who finds, by instinct, the clothes suited to her activities. She chooses lines appropriate to her daily tasks. The fashion designer then expands on this, develops these tendencies further. Contrary to what certain people might like to think, the movement does not happen from haute couture towards women, but the other way around. The fashion designer functions as a catalyst, he merely accentuates forms and colours. It always amuses me when I hear a designer say that he created such and such a line or garment. All he has done is sniff the air and his only genius lies in giving form to what was already there, a little ahead in time, perhaps, of what would be a general trend anyway.

Why does the length of dresses vary in cyclical fashion? Periodically the hem falls to the ankles . . . then up it goes again to the thighs. Could this be a pendular movement encouraged by haute couture? The answer is, 'No'. Does a designer say: 'Last season skirts were short, this year they will be long'? This would be granting them much too much power.

One could, of course, see in these fluctuations the simple expression of a greater or lesser moral freedom, with extreme expressions, such as, for example, Victorian dresses and the mini-skirt of the 1960s. But this explanation has never completely satisfied me. Because everything that is visible is symbolic, I have always thought that there must be a deeper reason for this phenomenon. By carefully observing fashions in relationship with the time they come to fruition, I had an idea – about 30 years ago. It was that clothes have a prophetic quality. I noticed, for example, that in prosperous times, women's dresses are very short. The family cocoon being safeguarded, she can go about in the world, her two legs free to wander. By contrast, when the unity of the family is threatened by unfavourable economic conditions, clothes become longer, below the knee. The curtain comes down. One could have fun studying the curve of economic crises compared with the length of skirts.

After the First World War, the West lived through the euphoric 'crazy years', boosted by radiant prosperity and the triumph of industrialization. Garments were light and very short. Nevertheless, in 1927 Jeanne Lanvin brutally lengthened skirts down to the ankles. Women covered their heads with large-brimmed hats. Two years later, the stock exchange crashed. Black Thursday happened and an international crisis began which resulted in the Second World War.

In 1950 world scientists and eminent personalities met at the Club of Rome to study what the post-war period would hold and what consequences technical evolution would have for science and world economy. The conclusions were extremely optimistic. They predicted a rosy future: techno-logical progress would finally bring happiness to all humanity. In the years that followed, women's clothes became shorter and shorter. The 1960s saw the advent of the mini-skirt. All fashion designers, led by Courrèges, were producing short dresses and skirts. Then, suddenly, in 1967, hems plunged, and Christian Dior launched his famous cossack coats. The following year, the big student revolts of May 1968 occurred and at the beginning of the 1970s, petrol prices rocketed followed by economic recession. After the optimistic predictions of the Club of Rome, this was a rude awakening! In effect, those brilliant economists had neglected to take into consideration the growing unease of the populations faced with technological development. They had forgotten to take into consideration the other side of the coin which included such frightening results as large-scale pollution. They disregarded the possibility that progress would be achieved at the expense of developing countries, an exploitation which would generate a massive population migration, a flux which would go from poor to rich countries, with predictable clashes such as the racism and growing xenophobia which we experience today. Yet these threats had somehow been intuitively expressed by fashion.

Every time a fashion designer has wanted to go against the current, he has failed. Creators do not just follow their whims. A good designer is not necessarily an inventor, but the one who discovers and anticipates evolutionary trends. He must constantly question what goes on around him, even the smallest phenomenon is of interest. Why is it, for example, that belts are worn very tight at times and are, at other times, eliminated altogether? By examining contemporary values, I have come to the conclusion that a woman 'tightens her belt' during puritanical periods. She is symbolically separating her brain from her sex. On the contrary, when there is great sexual freedom, belts are discarded and straight dresses come back into fashion. By the same token, the shape of shoulders is very revealing of prevailing attitudes. Why do women periodically feel the need to widen their shoulders by putting shoulder pads under their jackets or coats? I see it as a need to assert themselves, an acceptance of responsibilities, a demand for an active role in society and the refusal to give in to a male-oriented society. Square shoulders make a come-back when we are confronted with a crisis, such as a war for example: think of those years during the Cold War and the padding added to dresses, coats and jackets on the eve of the Gulf War.

I also refuse to see the changing height of feminine hairstyles as a gratuitous game. An example which comes to mind is that of Marie Antoinette. At the end of the 18th century, the hairstyles called 'à la Belle Poule' (Beautiful Hen) or 'Belle-Frégate' (Beautiful Frigate) were of considerable stature, reaching sometimes 1m in height. I suggest the following interpretation: the stability of a political regime is inversely proportional to the height of hairstyles. This hypothesis can be sustained by concrete examples. Marie Antoinette gave herself airs of grandeur, while sustaining a hairstyle which was easily the highest in the world (measuring 1m 20cm!): she was beheaded by the guillotine and the monarchy with her!

One can see the same coincidence between the 1830 and 1848 hairstyles and the revolutionary riots which took place during those years. Closer to our time, in 1956–7 we had the famous 'cucumbers' popularized by Brigitte Bardot. A year later, General de Gaulle was called to the presidency of the Council and the Fourth Republic was substituted by the Fifth. Soon after, hair becomes straight and disciplined again.

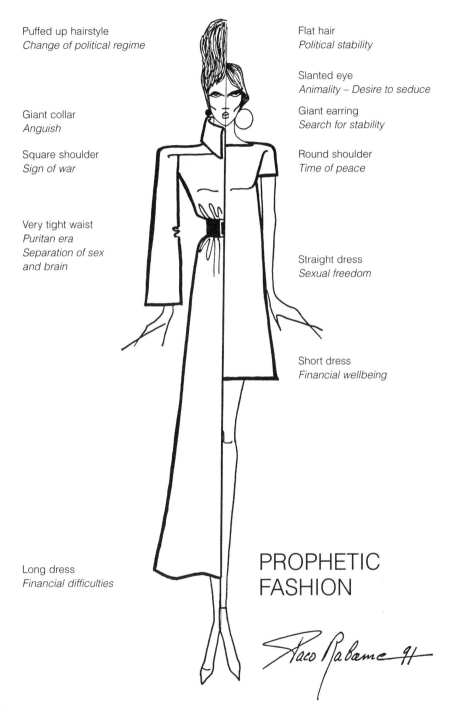

Puffed up hairstyle
Change of political regime

Flat hair
Political stability

Slanted eye
Animality – Desire to seduce

Giant collar
Anguish

Giant earring
Search for stability

Square shoulder
Sign of war

Round shoulder
Time of peace

Very tight waist
Puritan era
Separation of sex
and brain

Straight dress
Sexual freedom

Short dress
Financial wellbeing

Long dress
Financial difficulties

PROPHETIC
FASHION

Politicians would do well to ponder on these observations. If they want to measure the chances their regimes have, let them look at women's hairstyles.

Now, at the beginning of the 90s, hairstyles are becoming puffed up again: a sure sign that the present political regime does not have long to go. I would not be at all surprised if, in a few years, France underwent a troubled period leading to the establishment of a different regime, which would be neither to the right nor to the left. To know more, we can consult the prophecies of Nostradamus. His book entitled *Centuries* consists of rhymed quatrains grouped in hundreds, each set of 100 called a century. Century 2, quatrain 57 states:

> Before conflict the great wall will fall
> The great will die a sudden and painful death
> . . . most will swim
> Near the bloody river the earth is tainted

A quatrain which in 1991 made complete sense! As far as the following is concerned, I would do well not to interpret it (Century 3, quatrain 55):

> In the year when an eye in France will reign
> The court will be in serious trouble
> The grandee of Bloys his friend will kill
> Harming the reign and suspicion doubled

This analytic method is more intuitive than rational and I will apply it later to my own creations. What is the meaning of the use of metal, which has become an emblem of Paco Rabanne's fashion? For several decades now, everything around us has been made of metal, both in architecture and in sculpture – from Gustave Eiffel's work to César's sculptures. All the healing methods used by the present pharmaceutical products are based on metallic ions, be they homeopathic or oligo-elements or classical medicines. Everything which kills is metallic, from the gun's bullet to the atomic bomb, for uranium and plutonium are metals. After the stone age and the bronze age, we come to our own era, the steel age, or as the Hindus call it, the Kali-Yuga, which started some 6,000 years ago. It is the age during which there will be an extreme condensation of matter. By revesting women with metal, I was greeting the beginning of the end of the age of steel.

But from a social point of view, my first collection also corresponded to the birth of the women's liberation movement, which claimed for itself, among other things, equal pay and equal responsibilities. To cover women in chain armour, was like turning them into heroines like Joan of Arc and Amazons – warriors who oppose men's cowardice. On the whole, they understood the message perfectly. Those dresses had enormous success and the more aggressive and violent my creations, the better they sold. If they 'found' their public, it means they were resonant with people's objectives. In other words, if the use of metal had such an impact, it is because it corresponded to a particular moment of our spiritual and social evolution.

Recently, without abandoning my favourite material, metal, I have associated it with leather, for I feel that aggression is less the order of the day than it was in the 1960s, a time when artists on the whole were at their most violent. But I have not abandoned that metal, it still has its place and is still favoured sometimes. Many young designers include it in their collections today. We are closing the Kali-Yuga era and preparing to enter a new golden era. But all the ancient texts warn us: before entering this Edenic era, humanity will be subjected to some very difficult tests, cruel trials which we can already see foreshadowed.

During the 1950s, the Club of Rome had announced that technological progress, in particular where transportation was concerned, would reduce distances and the planet would 'shrink': people would travel around the world, they would take the aeroplane as they once took the train. So they could travel light, disposable clothes would be invented which could be bought in automatic machines, just like cigarettes, in airport halls. Modern man would have a disposable ready-to-wear wardrobe, from bathing suits to ball gowns.

But this idea was only viable if these clothes were sold cheaply. Therefore, one had to use the cheapest material, paper. In these years of abundance and dishevelled consumerism, paper has become a major competitor in the market; handkerchiefs, towels, tablecloths and sometimes even sheets resembling our grandmothers' cotton sheets are now made with paper. That fragile material seems to me to symbolize our happy-go-lucky civilization which has glorified the ephemeral. After numerous tests, I chose a type of paper used in military hospitals, soft, silent, uncreaseable, fireproof, practically tearproof and which could be washed once or twice.

With the help of a French manufacturer, Annick Roblin from Roanne (a French town in the Loire valley specializing in textiles and metallurgy), I was able to produce paper clothes which were sold in sachets for 15 francs. They had immediate success, particularly because we proposed dresses in gold or silver paper. Women were seduced by the idea of buying a fancy garment, for a small price, in which they could shine for one night. They found it quite erotic. What barrier could be more fragile than paper? With a similar perspective, I created a wedding dress for the daughter of the director of the chain-store Galeries Lafayette. She was married dressed entirely in white paper, embroidered with paper flowers. A wedding is a unique ceremony to which paper is perfectly suited, to my mind. One could imagine a whole market for paper pyjamas and nightdresses for large hotel chains.

But the events of 1968 dealt a fatal blow to the disposable dress. For as soon as there is a crisis, one witnesses a return to noble materials such as silk or satin. When the weather is fine, one dresses in 'a little rag', but as soon as dark clouds gather, one takes refuge in surer values. The more fragile a civilization, the more it holds on to traditions. The dress made of paper was not in symbiosis with the historic moment. No doubt it was ahead of its time. Today, young creators are toying with the idea again.

The paper dress had seduced me because it had a rare feature, only one seam. Western man is a slave to his costume, he is bound by all the stitches which hold together the multiple parts which make up his garment. In antiquity, or in certain Oriental civilizations, man wore simple drapes as clothes. I was taken with the desire to push the idea further and create a garment entirely without seams. That is how I became interested in a moulding technique invented by a French engineer. All one has to do is to fashion mannequins in iron sheets corresponding to the different feminine sizes. The mannequin mould is dipped in a bath of vinyl sodium chloride. Then, after taking off the mould, one obtains a one-piece garment which is cheap, flexible and like a second skin. The technical complexity of the procedure requires a large investment and no industrial baron is yet ready to take the risk. But one can see there a prefiguration of fashion for the year 2000.

Every creator is perforce an 'abnormal' being, that is to say, outside the norm: a tree which is taller than the others in the forest. He is an outsider, living on the edge of social taboos, outside social castes, he is not a slave to social mores and customs. He intuits future events. He is not content with daily routine and yearns for change. The majority of people also want everything to evolve, for evolution is part of the natural order of things and will remain so, from the initial big bang to the final big bang, when the world ends. But the desires of the public form a kind of inchoate mass, incapable of expressing itself clearly and even less capable of taking shape in concrete form. This is where creative people come in: they perceive the aspirations of the group and give them shape, each in his own field and with the appropriate support, be it with books, paintings or clothes. The masses adopt these innovations with delight and integrate them with great ease, for they meet an expectation. But the universal psyche always asks for more, seeking to satisfy new desires, to fulfil a void left by its own evolution.

Creation is, and will remain, continuous. The pessimists, the envious and other prophets of doom periodically announce the death of haute couture; they nurture an illusion. For the demand of the public is, by its very nature, insatiable. There will always be creative people to give form to that demand, people capable of finding new sources of inspiration, whispered by the gods in the artist's ear or produced by an exacerbated sensitivity.

I have often had the opportunity to see painter friends at work. They settle down a few feet away from a large white canvas and remain very still for some long minutes, some-times for hours, as if hypnotized by that immaculate surface. Suddenly they go forward, as in a trance, their hand makes broad gestures marking the canvas with sweeping lines. In a hypnotic state they start drawing lines and throwing colour on the canvas. Suddenly they stop, regain their composure and look at the canvas: 'Did I do that?' They do not understand what they have just sketched. The following day they confront the canvas again to contemplate that mysterious draft until the fire of inspiration takes hold of them once more. This inspiration is that of the famous Greek Muses, the sacred lyre, the sacred anger which animates creative people.

A minor art, fashion does not know such divine fire, but fashion designers can hear celestial music. Creativity demands total concentration, the effacement of the ego, the dissolution of the personality. One has to forget oneself and become receptive to that kind of vibration, that inner light which is inspiration. And suddenly the hand starts moving, as if possessed by a strange feminine force. For inspiration is feminine, from the celestial Mother, the creative earth which makes trees grow, to the woman who gives birth to a child. Man is action, he provides the impulse, but it is the woman who is truly creative.

I sometimes seek inspiration in my past lives, or rather, when I detach from my ego, my past lives come to the surface. One day I was doodling mechanically on a sheet of paper, when I recognized with surprise that the sketch was clearly of Egyptian inspiration. I continued to draw, letting my fingers guide the pencil. In no time, I had drawn an Egyptian low-relief.

When I start to work, it is first of all the lower mental functioning, the intellect, which labours and my drawings are unsatisfactory, they don't flow and they lack grace. As I persist, little by little an empty mental space is created within me and I feel myself becoming a reed. I feel inhabited by another self or a self which is conscious that his body is only one of many envelopes. My drawings improve, become more creative. The superior mental functioning connects with the sixth energy level, the level of knowledge and of memories. All those memories of women whom I met or loved in the past, are recollections I update and mix with visions of the future.

Although each creator is receptive to his inspiration, the designer must never, under any circumstances, impose his fashion: he must be content to propose it. Each human being must ardently defend his personality and refuse to follow the crowd. During the 1960s I spoke violently against the dictatorship of fashion designers. I was not alone. Hélène Lazareff in her magazine, *Elle*, made an effort to launch some 'stylists', creative designers who were not in the world of high fashion and who allowed women to become free of the dictatorship of haute couture. At the time, I voiced very prejudiced opinions, which were misinterpreted. I said, for example, that a woman who follows fashion is an imbecile. The journalists who eagerly took hold of that declaration, often omitted the rest of the sentence: '. . . an imbecile because a woman should not be servile to fashion, fashion should serve her'. Each designer offers possibilities, women must make their choice according to their physical attributes, their personalities, their desires. By doing this, they avoid being confined to the role of 'object', a role in which women have been incarcerated for too long. She should not serve clothes, the clothes should serve her and enhance her qualities. It is she who must make use of them and refuse to be a slave to fashion. Therefore, I put myself in an ambiguous situation. I went into the world of haute couture saying to women: 'Don't follow fashion, create your own style!'

I still denounce some of my colleagues who seem to fantasize to the detriment of women. I consider that a creative designer has all the rights, except that of ridiculing women, which is exactly what some of them do. To me that is a crime against the profession and against human beings. One can stretch the imagination, make women into goddesses, extraterrestrials, princesses, queens or schoolgirls, but under no circumstances should one vilify their image.

To dress a woman is also to make her seductive, allowing her to respond to men's fantasies. I hope, in not too distant a future, men will also be dressed in ways which fulfil women's dreams! They will be successively sailor, fighter, business man and many other characters and will no longer wear uniforms and be so boring to look at! However, it seems that the woman of the 1990s has liberated herself from fashion, in the positive sense. She takes whatever suits her personality, which is exactly as it should be. My concept of fashion is the very opposite of an obligation. Clothes should be a means for the personality to bloom.

To put an end to fashion dictatorship, we must concentrate on human beings and their deepest nature. For if fashion is a reflection of the sacred and the social aspects of human life, it also reflects people's psychology. Dress expresses and betrays existential problems. If a man is not in harmony with his work, if he is in conflict with his family, if he has a problem with the woman he loves or with his children, this is going to show in the way he dresses. He will choose a style of clothes, a colour, which will act like a shield or a banner for his rebellion. He is conveying, in this way, something which he cannot verbalize.

As soon as there is a problem, a person who normally has a 'classical' taste will show slightly different preferences, adding a touch of audacity. She or he will wear this accessory like a symbol, a form of provocation: a rather loud tie, something a bit decadent. Women will choose a very showy piece of jewellery, an exuberant hairstyle. The woman who wears 15 bracelets on her arms has serious problems: she is afraid she will be neglected or not loved, therefore she will noisily wave her trinkets around, as if to say: 'I am here, I exist, look at me, love me'. On the other hand, a woman who is loved and who knows it will wear light and discreet jewellery. The deeper the problem, the more extreme will be the provocation. For the punks, there is no future, no survival. So they spit on their era, wearing shapeless clothes, dyeing their hair green, red, or orange, sporting safety pins which they use, not on their clothes, but on their own flesh, as if to sacrifice it.

One says, perhaps too lightly, that appearances are deceptive. We have seen how being and seeming cannot be disassociated, nor can microcosm and macrocosm. Everything is symbolic. Having said this, it is of course true that the deepest quest overcomes by far the simple observation of human behaviour. The visible, although extremely revealing, is but a stage which should invite us to go further, into a deeper and much more exacting quest.

5

Beyond Tangible Forms

❧❦❧

He saw too much. And seeing is blinding
TRISTAN CORBIÈRE

To know at last – to know the hidden truth, to know ourselves, guess our future and discover the meaning of our existence: that is what tempts us all, believers, agnostics and atheists alike, in spite of what we might say. Well, the material world offers us many bridges which can lead us to the other side of things, beyond the world we know. Everything seems to encourage us not to be content with appearances, but to look for 'the things which lie behind things'. But how should we conduct that quest without falling into a cheap esoteric delirium?

Astrology, geomancy, clairvoyance, fortune-telling: there are so many ways of trading with the invisible. More and more people resort to these methods, hoping to find a solution to their daily problems or answers to existential questions. But that 'commerce' with the beyond is, more often than not, a money-grabbing affair rather than true communication. Some people abuse those techniques, as if they were absolutely necessary to our spiritual search; others are wary, because they fear impostors or because they see these areas as darkly mysterious and full of disquieting rituals. But the journey the initiate undertakes is a quest to unravel the mysterious, the enigma of one's own being. The knowledge which he will have access to is necessarily secret. And what is secret makes us touch the sacred. These sciences, whatever their degree of authenticity, manipulate very real, all-powerful forces.

Early man lived in a world of countless dangers; he was at the mercy of wild animals and of the elements which threatened his survival. Conscious of his vulnerability, he lived in terror of the dark. It is in this feeling of fear that one must look for the origins of religion. Confronted with permanent external threats, man discovered, first of all, simple means of protection: he warded off danger by wearing talismans or amulets. Since he was unable to fight these gigantic forces, he preferred to tame them. The sun and the storms became gods; bears and wild boars became totems.

In order to protect himself from wild beasts and inclement weather, man found refuge in caves, which is to say, in the earth's belly. He then created, by analogy, feminine deities like the Virgins of Lespugue and Willendorf. These women protected him in the night, as the mother shelters her child in her belly. Then he thought about how he could have a harmonious relationship with the powers that surrounded him. How could he earn their good graces? What object could he use to seduce them, with what technique, what gesture or sound? How could he predict and control natural events?

From these questions, operational magic was born. Sorcerers appeared, claiming to know rituals which acted on these phenomenons. Gradually, they decreed the laws which would rule the group. For social rules originate from magical laws, imposed not by the chief of the village, but by the sorcerer. These magic rituals and this cult of natural divinities progressively became a religion. Man had access to abstraction when he imagined, for the first time, that all of nature's violent manifestations obey some superior force, that they are commanded by some unique, colossal power. This marked the arrival of *Homo sapiens* and the entry into the third energy level in which we are still living today.

I went through my first apprenticeship in operational magic while observing my grandmother, who claimed she had inherited her secrets from the ancient druids. When we lived in Brittany, there was no doctor or chemist in the nearest market town. My grandmother healed the neighbouring population with plants. She prescribed infusions, decoctions and poultices. Case by case, she taught me the effects that plants have on the human body. She told me that each plant corresponded in its shape to the organ it could heal. The roots, the stem and the leaf have very different virtues. The part buried in the earth does not have the same power as the part which opens to the sun. The roots scour the earth, absorb its moisture and mineral salts. The leaf, on the contrary, dilates, ascends towards the sun. Everything that is under the ground has a contracting effect on the human body, everything that is in the open air has a dilating effect.

When an organ suffers a lesion, it often means that it has grown bigger or smaller and one can remedy this imbalance with plants, being careful not to upset the body's natural cycles. In fact, organs open and close according to the hours of the day and of the night. The whole universe obeys these laws of contraction and dilation. This is also true of human psychology: hope dilates the heart, envy dries it out. My grandmother repeatedly said that the body and nature function in the same way and it is sufficient to observe one to know the other. Every affliction finds its remedy in nature, for God has put everything at our disposal. Therefore, what we call 'magical practices' are, in fact, the applied knowledge of the laws which govern the world. It is the understanding of the deep, hidden causes, whereas 'official' science, the so-called positive science in the sense of palpable, is but the limited knowledge of certain laws by their visible consequences, the symptoms.

The mistrust which magic inspires is often based on ignorance. Learned materialists reject these practices which they associate with superstition. But magic, when it is finally studied, will become a science. Scientists are only just beginning to take an interest in certain plants used by African sorcerers and voodoo magicians. Homeopathy has recently been accepted, but the scientific community has not yet understood the power of plants, of stones, of sounds and of gestures. They do in fact use crystals in electronic devices, but without having complete understanding of their powers. And when we don't know something, it is so much easier to classify it as superstition. When the secrets of nature reveal themselves to us in this way, little by little, we are invaded by a feeling of wonder. How could we not be in awe of the possibilities of the human body? When I had my first experience in spiritualism I was amazed by the power of my magnetism.

Our first meeting with this other reality leaves us in a fantastic state of exaltation. One discovers a new and enticing world and wants to know more; one throws oneself wholeheartedly into this quest, convinced it is the best road to take. We do not know that it is precisely where great dangers await us; for esoteric research is a path which, even when started upon as fun, is never innocent. By embarking on it we are, in fact, appealing to subtle energies which exist. They are very real and, if we are not careful in our dealings with those energies, they can burn our wings.

My first steps in this super-sensitive world were some seances in that Russian lady's home, when I was living in Sables d'Olonne. She taught me how to 'make the tables turn'. She also taught me the ouija-board technique. The board is a wooden disc with an arrow in the middle and on its circumference an alphabet is set out. One makes the pointer of the arrow turn, repeating the operation many times, at an accelerated pace, until words are spelt, giving answers to the question we ask. This technique, which is close to automatic writing, is apparently harmless. But one must know when to stop, for by always wanting to find answers outside oneself, there is the risk of sacrificing one's capacity for initiative and action. In a similar vein, I have numerous friends who went blindly into the study of yoga postures to awaken their chakras.

It is quite true that by certain gestures, taught by yoga, one can activate in oneself the opening of certain organs, allow the descent of cosmic energies and, thereby, provoke a certain inner realignment. But, unfortunately, in the majority of cases, the spirit is not sufficiently prepared. The apprentices have not sufficiently mastered the techniques required for the redistribution of those energies when they are brought into the body. Consequently, one sees numerous yogi apprentices burn, not their wings, but their organs: in effect, these new forces are dispersed within the body in a completely uncontrolled way.

In India, the true masters, who know the science of yoga perfectly, have a different mentality, another approach. They know that it is both a spiritual and a physical practice. They can, therefore, control those energies and know how to use them to increase their receptivity. But in Europe, there are countless people who bruise their bodies wanting to practise yoga as one does warm-up exercises. Worse, they practise yoga because it is fashionable or exotic, whereas these are 'magical' practices, destined to heighten our perception of outer and inner phenomena.

We live in a material world which is a succession of forms. These forms emit a vibration and thus exert upon us a force of attraction or repulsion. Everything in nature is either positive or negative, dilation or contraction, feminine or masculine, terrestrial or celestial, shadow or light. If we accumulate negative energies in ourselves, we run the risk of destroying our nervous and lymphatic systems. A surcharge of positive energies is also harmful, for the input of badly controlled dilating forces can provoke lesions in our system. Balance and measure are essential rules both for good health and wisdom. According to the tradition of Sufism, the one who searches, the one who wants to go through the small door leading to the reign of knowledge, must first cross the Shira bridge, a path which is narrower than the blade of the yatagan, the short Arab sabre. One has to walk barefoot on the sword's edge. If one falls to the right, one goes mad, if one falls to the left, the soul is destroyed. It is the most terrible of deaths, spiritual death, annihilation.

Like all the forces which animate the cosmos, our thoughts too can be positive or negative. Each one emits a vibration. When our spirit concentrates on one person, she or he can feel it, for our thought-wave will come and touch her. That wave will then rebound towards us! Like boomerangs, the thought-waves, be they good or bad, come back to their point of departure: thus the danger of witchcraft which makes use of foul thoughts. Those who practise black magic, seeking to harm (in contrast with white magic, which aims at improvement), run the risk that the flame will return to destroy them. I will illustrate this by telling you a rather surprising but perfectly true anecdote, which will illustrate very well this principle of thought-boomeranging!

I have always been attracted by different cultures (while knowing that I must remain faithful to mine) and I frequently go to exotic restaurants in Paris such as African, Chinese or Japanese. Some years ago, I became friends with a French woman who owned an African restaurant. She had a close friend from Benin who was the author of a famous book on magic. Benin is a country where these activities are very popular and Brazilian *macumba* is thought to originate either from there or from Haitian voodoo. Due to circumstances which I cannot recall, I fell out with this young woman. Her friend sided with her and took a dislike to me.

I awoke one night sweating as if I had just had a nightmare. I felt very hot then very cold, by turns. Sitting up in my bed, I was terrified to see green flames licking the ceiling all around my room. Thanks to the lessons my grandmother had given me, I immediately understood what was happening. Someone was exercising witchcraft skills on me! Repressing my panic, I tried to concentrate. I asked: 'Who are you? What do you want?' While I meditated in silence, I saw before me the face of that sorcerer from Benin. He was casting a spell on me, probably with the help of a doll fashioned in my image.

I decided to teach him a lesson. Simply by using my thought-power, I transformed myself into a mirror, an immense mirror. I no longer existed as a physical body, I was simply a reflector. I sent that man a positive thought, a love thought. 'Listen! I am a mirror. A mirror that loves you. Everything you wish me, I return it to you a thousand times'. I stayed like that for an hour or two. Suddenly the phone rang. It was my sorcerer: 'Paco, Paco, stop! I beg you! I won't do it again! Please . . .' He had understood that, thanks to my mirror of love, I had returned his negative thoughts and these had boomeranged back to hit him. With his thoughts returned to him, he stopped immediately.

It is, in fact, the principle of the Basque ball game played with a soft ball made of string or leather. It is a magic sport, an Atlantean game as old as time played by four players, the four elements or the four branches of the swastika. Armed with his *chistera*, the player throws the ball onto the wall with tremendous force. The ball hits the surface which opposes it with inertia and the ball comes back to the other players, redoubling its force. The Basque cross is engraved on the pediment, its four arms bent like commas. It is the famous swastika also used by the American Indians; they too are escapees from the cataclysm which swallowed up Atlantis. It is the symbol of the vortex of creation, of the development of the universe around the fixed point which is God. It is the Nazi cross, with the difference that Hitler used it in the inverse gyrating sense: the positive rotations became negative and the swastika was then transformed into a symbol of destruction.

I do not believe that the malevolent forces which operate in the universe are the devil's work. The devil, in my view, is no more real than hell. Or rather, in the same way that hell is right here on earth, the devil is us; it is the result of negative thoughts emitted by men. It is not God but man who created the devil! At the beginning God separated light from dark. Man reintroduced darkness and gave it form in the shape of Satan.

However, let us not confuse Satan and Lucifer. Lucifer means the one who carries the light. Keeper of the secret knowledge, represented by the emerald which he carried encrusted in the middle of his forehead, Lucifer was God's favourite angel and the one most devoted to him. For the love of God and creation, but no doubt also due to pride, he came to earth to bring knowledge to a humanity which had been buried in material darkness since Adam's fall, guilty of having turned away from God. But is one allowed to seize God's light in this way, even with good intentions? A lot has been written about Lucifer and this is only my personal interpretation. According to the legend and sacred texts, it seems that this descent to earth rendered Lucifer, temporarily, a fallen angel. His self-conceit is perhaps the reason for the way in which the science he was bringing was adulterated.

The sacred writings tell us that, during his fall, he lost his emerald. It was inside the emerald that, according to Arthurian legend, the Holy Grail was carved, the cup in which Joseph of Arimathæa collected Christ's blood. But, parallel to this, the men to whom Lucifer brought light, perverted that light: they made of it a positivist science first, and then secondly the adulterated inspiration of sorcerers' apprentices. From that time onwards Lucifer has been endowed with a negative value and has become the inspiration for all those who pursue malevolent powers. One finds that ambivalence in the myth of Prometheus, who stole a spark of fire from Zeus to bring it to earth. By offering men the divine spirit, fire, he imbued them with the overweening desire to rival the gods. The sorcerer's apprentice is often secretly animated by the desire to become a superman. But by practising magic, he is playing with fire.

As soon as we become conscious that there is a higher order, a superior world, we want to familiarize ourselves with it at all costs, to master the techniques which will open its doors and will allow us to influence both our earthly life and that of others. From time immemorial, man has wanted to unravel the secrets of the distant past or of the future: the Roman haruspex, for example, the soothsayer who sacrificed animals and divined the will of the gods by examining their entrails; palmistry which interprets the lines of the hand; geomancy which reads the signs on the ground; necromancy which evokes the dead to obtain revelations; and fortune-tellers who think they might obtain revelations with playing cards.

It would be too easy to dismiss these methods as vulgar tricks, but these means of divination are real! The more one progresses with meditation, and the purification of negative energies, the more one is free of the mental litter which separates man from nature, the more powers descend into one. At first, one feels dazzled. Imagine how you would feel if you suddenly discovered you could read the thoughts of people around you; that you could tell a person's destiny by dealing tarot cards! Once that stage is reached, many people consider themselves satisfied, glad to be able to astonish and dominate. From that moment on, they stop halfway on their inner quest, that path which should take them up to the stage where they forget themselves, to total humility. By discovering the power of operational magic, they seek to master it and quickly open shop. But to do business with one's knowledge in that field is not without its dangers. One can put one's gifts at the service of others and, if necessary, ask for something in return, but one should not use them to acquire a fortune or power over others. For then it is our soul we are selling and losing.

Even without wanting to trade in these powers, it is wise, if one possesses them, to remain prudent. I know, because I have used those powers. I have made objects change place, I have made tables turn, read other people's thoughts, been tempted to astonish friends and strangers by demonstrating how reliable those techniques are! I have used my gifts to draw people's attention, to seduce. There lies the great temptation: to use one's gifts for personal ends. That is a trap which is set out for us, the ambush which emerges from the shadows to trip the foolhardy ones who try to cross the Shira bridge with impure intentions.

One has to look further, go forward on the path of knowledge, ask for the impossible and become excessive: mad about God. One has to say: 'Since he possesses that colossal intelligence which rules the world and now that I have had a glimpse of those laws, it is that ultimate intelligence which I want to know. I want to experience that folly of wishing to contemplate the one and merge with it'. Then the magical powers wither, or rather what disappears is the desire to debase them. They are within us, as if forgotten. Then the path opens before us, brighter. New lights are offered us, we hear the call of our inner voice, of our conscience telling us: 'Don't do that, do this! Go in this direction! Open this book!' But it is not our conscience, it is a guide sent to us by the gods who are at our side, sometimes within us. He advises us on our long path, filled with traps and yet so simple.

It often takes a lifetime for that simplicity to be revealed to us, such is the slowing down of our evolution due to our genetic heredity, family, schooling, social environment and the complexity of our own personality. I have myself taken numerous misleading paths. I have gone right and left, I have fallen into impasses or suddenly felt myself cut off from God, in a terrible mental and moral desert. But I did not drown, I did not lose my faith. I simply understood that I had taken the wrong path and, retracing my steps, I started again, trying to pay more attention to my inner voice. It is during silent meditation, in that appeal that one sends to the one saying: 'I love You, You who created the universe', it is with that cry of love that suddenly the energies descend and come to one's rescue. We have all known such moments, when we feel completely lost. What is essential then is to understand that an act of will is enough to remove the blockage. As soon as I take the first step in that direction, yesterday's hesitations are completely forgotten. The traveller who has just eaten his fill, does he think of the hunger he suffered the day before?

Everything is so simple! If only I had known, if only we knew! Years of tentative efforts are necessary. The one who succeeds in lifting Isis' veil is surprised to discover a second veil, then a third . . . The more we progress, the more truths we discover. We are then filled with a sacred fear, with a feeling of humility. For when we make a mistake, we are diverted from the divine plan, we are reprimanded: when we fall ill, when we have money problems, when our friends leave us. These are calls to order, of greater or lesser violence. When we go back to the path that was set out for us, everything becomes smooth again, everything becomes luminous. There is a kind of inner peace, a feeling of calm and joy. And then we know, without hesitation, that we are on the right track

Christ said 'Blessed are the poor in spirit'. Blessed are those who do not complicate things, because the truth is simple, one can never say it enough. One has to preserve in oneself the soul of a child and with it the capacity for wonder. Jesus said 'Suffer the little children to come unto me, for theirs is the kingdom of Heaven' (Matthew 19: 14).

The cynical reader will think: 'Simplicity, simplicity! Wouldn't our life be made much easier if we knew from the start the destiny assigned to us?'

Astrologers claim that they can unravel a person's fate by studying astral conjunctions. The Egyptians, the Tibetans, the Aztecs all practised astrology. The basic principle is the following: all living beings are subject to the influence of the stars. But that concept has degenerated into a simple, mechanistic determinism. To my eyes, the stars do not influence our destiny, yet they can indicate the guidelines. If you are an Aquarian, you are a dreamer, an idealist; if you are an Aries person, you are determined; if you are a Taurean you're a man full of energy, willpower and temper. The signs of the zodiac reveal our behaviour, our possibilities and our faults of character. We inherited, at birth, a life-plan which one can retrace by certain techniques. But we have the capacity to accelerate or slow down that plan.

Out of curiosity I studied astrology, became familiar with numerology and the tarot. But I don't use those techniques and have even renounced the use of my talents as a medium. I believe it is dangerous to consult clairvoyants too often, for one ends up by relinquishing one's own will in the process. It is a form of resignation from life. Nevertheless, from time to time, if we are faced with an important problem, if we have no friends to confide in, a visit to a clairvoyant may clarify things. He or she can show us new ways of approaching the problem and new perspectives. It's obvious that we should not go and see them every month to find out whether we are going to find a country home, obtain a pay rise or find the love of our life on the next street corner. At crucial moments in my life, when serious problems needed solving, when I've had to take important decisions regarding my career, I've consulted astrologers or clairvoyants. They gave me advice, which I took into consideration, sometimes following it, other times not. But they provided me with a different outlook which has sometimes been of help in sorting out a difficult situation.

When I came up to Paris to study at the Beaux Art school, for example, I felt that I was at a turning point in my life. I decided to consult a clairvoyant, more out of curiosity than conviction. I had read in the press that the best clairvoyant in Paris was Belline, who lived in Rue Fontaine. I went to see him. He welcomed me, dealt the cards and read the ink marks. He then announced that my success would come 'through women'. At the time I saw my future as an architect and immediately thought he was a bit mad. Success through women? Unless I became a pimp, I could not see how this prediction could come true! I told him my doubts.

He didn't waver. 'You will be working surrounded by women, and it is women who will make your fortune.'

I was almost annoyed by his insistence. He added: 'You will create something which looks a little like a book, at least in its outer form.'

With his two index fingers, he drew a triangle in space, about 15cm high. 'It is not very thick', he went on. 'It talks about metal, it is surrounded by metal. This object will go around the world and will bring you riches and fame.'

I left Belline's house hooting with laughter. For the first time in my life I had consulted a clairvoyant and he had told me the most incredible drivel.

Thirteen years later, I became a fashion designer. I worked surrounded by models and seamstresses. I created for women and was successful thanks to them. Then I launched my perfume named Calandre. The bottle is surrounded by metal, the size of a small book. Today, it is the best-selling French perfume, together with Pour Homme, all over the world.

The clairvoyants I consult from time to time immediately notice my mediumistic gifts. I reciprocate, for as soon as one of them goes into trance, I don't remain passive. Our spirits communicate, time stands still, there is a kind of interpenetration. At the end of these consultations, I myself have 'flashes' regarding the events that will affect these clairvoyants within the next few months. Many decades ago, when I was still studying architecture, I went to see a clairvoyant who lives near the Étoile. We sat at a table. Suddenly a dazzling light made me wince. I thought at first that it was a ray of sunshine shining on my face, but that light seemed to have no particular source, it came from every side all at once. Then a smell of lilies and roses filled the room. A heady perfume which made me almost dizzy. 'Why are you burning such strong incense?' I asked. 'And what is that light?'

'I'm not burning incense', said the clairvoyant, looking very disturbed. 'There is an intense light behind you. That's where the luminosity and the perfume are coming from. It seems to be benevolent towards you.'

Those light-filled entities are our guides, our guardian angels sent by God. At the moment of creation there were different levels in the materialization of the supreme energy. The celestial hierarchies which, in the Judeo-Christian cosmos, correspond to these levels are organized by seven angelic orders: thrones, cherubs, seraphs and so on. These are spiritual, ethereal beings which act as intermediaries between God and the world. When one has mediumistic gifts or when one is advanced in meditation, these angels sometimes appear. They are like breaths of fresh air which cross the room, caressing one's face with a refreshing tenderness although the windows and doors are closed. They want to signal their presence, as if to say: 'Don't forget, we are with you.' They are called 'masters of light'. But we must remember this: they can only intervene in our life if we surrender our free will. In order to obtain their help, we have to give up that exorbitant power. Then, everything becomes easy! These messengers of God say to the initiates, 'When you take one step towards us, we take ten in your direction.' 'Ten steps towards you . . .' What we take for 'intuition' is often the intervention of these celestial beings. Which one among us has not heard that voice, whispering, advising us as to which direction to take, warning us against an imminent danger? Even the most Cartesian individuals, who would rather eliminate that intruder, end up by listening to these pleas. Somehow they know, baffled, that it protects them.

When my father was made prisoner and the whole of the Basque country threatened to fall to the Francoist regime, my mother decided to leave Spain, knowing she risked execution. We, my mother, my grandmother, my two sisters, my brother and I, managed to reach the town of San Sebastián, which was caught in a stranglehold. We boarded the last ship leaving for Mexico. It was full of Republicans running away from the civil war and the repression led by the Falangists. In the general confusion, the whistle for departure sounded. Suddenly, as the gangway was being lifted, my mother screamed. She didn't want to stay on board! She wanted to get down immediately! Dragging her children and my protesting grandmother, my mother hurried onto the gangway and insisted that we be allowed to get off. Furious, the captain finally yielded.

Standing on the pier, we watched the boat sailing away from San Sebastián. My grandmother was cursing against this sudden folly:

'You're mad! The Falangists will be invading this town any minute now! You have just let our last chance of survival slip through our fingers!'

As the boat was reaching the open sea, a loud roar filled the skies. Turning our heads, we saw a German air patrol. They had seen the ship and immediately took it as a target. Hit by several bombs, the ship sank in a few seconds under our horrified gaze. There were no survivors.

My grandmother was flabbergasted. We didn't even have time to ponder on that drama and my mother's extraordinary intuition for a truck stopped a few yards from us.

'Are you trying to get away from San Sebastián?' asked the driver. 'I will take you. I know a safe route.'

Hidden under some sacks at the back of the truck, we were able to outmanoeuvre the Falangist roadblocks and proceed to Barcelona, which was still held by the Republicans. Heaven was watching over the Cuervo family.

In February 1939, Barcelona fell to the Falangists and we left, travelling on foot through the mountains to reach France. One night, we found shelter from the snow in a half-ruined house. In the middle of the night, my mother suddenly woke up.

'They killed him! They have killed my husband!' she cried.

She burst into tears. I tugged at her skirt.

'Don't worry, I am here. From now on, I will be your husband.'

It was only thanks to my grandmother's soothing care that my mother was convinced to go back to bed. The next day we continued on our journey. Later, in France, we received the notification of my father's death. It had happened the very day my mother had had that premonition. My mother – so Cartesian!

My grandmother initiated me in the art of dream interpretation. According to her, there were three kinds of dream. The first, the most inoffensive, is the digestion dream. After a heavy meal, our stomach being somewhat upset, we will have nonsensical visions, dreams with no particular message. Then, there are the compensatory dreams, typically Freudian. The young virgin who dreams that a man is persecuting her with a big knife; or the office clerk who is bullied by his hierarchical superior and who dreams that he is a masked avenger who cuts his boss into pieces. Finally there is the premonitory dream, represented by the black man upside down, head down, feet up in the air. A symbol which means we must read dreams upside down.

If you dream that your mother is dying and that the blood is pouring out of her wound, you must not worry. On the contrary, your mother is very healthy, because death, in that inverted world, means life. And that blood which is oozing out

INVOLUTION

EVOLUTION

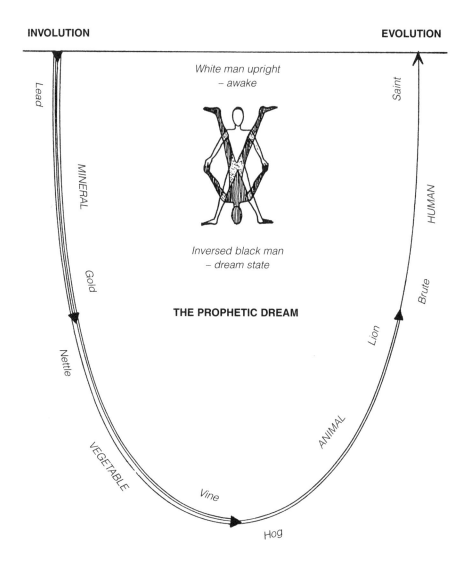

Lead

MINERAL

Gold

Nettle

VEGETABLE

Vine

Hog

ANIMAL

Lion

Brute

HUMAN

Saint

*White man upright
– awake*

*Inversed black man
– dream state*

THE PROPHETIC DREAM

KARMIC ENERGY
PROGRESSION

Paco Rabanne 91

of a wound is a large sum of money which will swell her bank account!

One day, a woman came to see my grandmother, saying:

'I had a strange dream: I was writing a letter. My son approached the table I was writing on, he took the sheet, knocking over the inkpot and my son was covered in ink.'

My grandmother answered: 'Look after your son! He may well have health problems.'

When the woman left my grandmother said:

'That is precisely what I mean by a premonitory dream upside down. The woman is writing. The ink is what names, what gives life to things. The boy was covered by this life-giving liquid. Therefore, he is going to die.'

That very day, the child evaded the mother's supervision and crossed the street carelessly. He was run over by a car.

Dreams can also tell us about our past lives. For example, a landscape which comes back to us again and again, a town which repeatedly becomes the scenario for our dreams, or somebody we don't know in this world but who is a faithful companion in our walks in the realm of dreams. Those are places and people which have been important to us in the past, they gave us great joy or made us suffer and these experiences remain engraved in our memory.

Sleep can also take us to higher energy levels – on condition that we do not become terrified! We have all had that nightmare in which we are sucked down in an endless vertiginous fall. Sometimes the sleeper kicks the air in an attempt to climb up again. That dream corresponds to the moment when the ethereal body detaches from the body in order to float in space. But it falls again, for people don't know they can climb higher and the sensation frightens them! If they had the courage or wished to do so, they could travel into that luminous tunnel which leads to higher energy levels. Catherine Emmerich, a stigmatized nun, went on astral trips, visited unknown planets, relived past lives. Her amazing visions were recorded by both Clemens Brentano and Goethe.

Deep into the realm of the night, I'm sure that the reader is wondering now: what about our dear deceased, whom we catch a glimpse of in our dreams, sometimes feeling their presence? What about sleep, that 'twin brother of death'? And what about death itself, real death, often evoking dreadful terror and the inevitable question, what happens then?

When a human being dies, he leaves his physical body. But as he is not fully conscious that his envelope of flesh is dead, it takes a few days for the disincarnated soul to elevate itself. It floats around the body and tries to speak to people. That is why in numerous traditions there are professional mourners, who cry out loud. By their tears, they convey to the dead person that they are no longer of this world, that they no longer have any business here. Christians practise a magic ritual by putting four candles around the bed, thus creating a very powerful ascensional field which leads to the fourth level of existence, the realm of the dead.

The soul then goes through a silver tunnel – the same tunnel that I went through when I was seven years old, and which those who have been in a deep coma or 'near death' also experience. At the entrance to this luminous world, we are welcomed by the guardian of the threshold, a being of great purity whom the Christians identify as Jesus and the Muslims as Mohammed. He asks that terrible question:

'Man! What have you done in your life?'

You then see the whole of your life parade before you, the opportunities you had to do good and which were not taken, all the positive gestures in harmony with the divine plan which you were asked to perform to lighten your karma. That examination is totally impartial. There are no attenuating or aggravating circumstances, only reality.

And the judgement is made. Either we are condemned to a slow purification on the fourth energy level or, if we have been a good person, we go to the fifth level, or higher. When we wander in the realm of the dead, we can turn towards the brilliance of superior levels. But it also happens that we hear calls coming from earth: a being who asks, begs for help. We can then look down and, sometimes, even try to descend. But that movement is very difficult because it requires colossal energy. That is when we, who are on earth, feel those light breaths brush past us or those messages received when making the tables turn or through automatic writing.

But those spiritualist practices are not always advisable. We must mourn our dead, but without recalling them back to earth. We should think about them and say: 'Go up, elevate yourself towards the light! Cultivate only that desire!' If they protect us and we 'feel' it, apart from the delirium brought about by suffering or the imagination, it is because they are already beings of light who have reached the higher levels. But it is not up to us to ask. We must 'pray for them', says the simple and wise celebration. Pray that they may elevate themselves.

To elevate himself, the deceased has two possibilities, as we have seen. To progress very slowly while staying on the fourth level or to choose to reincarnate to improve himself on earth, to lighten his karma further. But before touching the body of that woman who will become his mother, he must 'drink the water of the river of forgetfulness'. Thus, when he is born, he has forgotten everything and must, slowly, follow Ariadne's thread.

Death is a stage. But there are many people who reject it, out of ignorance. This is particularly so for materialists who, at the moment of death, are often seized with panic, with fear of the void. They desperately hang on to matter, to all that they can see. Then their soul can no longer leave the third level; it attaches itself to a piece of furniture, to a wall, a room. Their body decomposes, returns to dust, but their soul remains locked in this earthly place which they then desperately try to depart from. Those lost souls, those 'ghosts' manage to appear, from time to time, through mediums. They take advantage of the energies which they emit to communicate their distress.

I have seen and felt numerous ghosts. Contrary to what is current in popular imagination, those beings bear no malevolent intentions. Their intervention in our lives are like cries for help. They want to free themselves and leave that intermediary place to pursue their evolutionary path. They realize the blindness in which a life of pure materialism held them. It is possible to help them! I have often intervened at the request of friends, who had their houses visited by these noisy 'spirits'.

A famous French fashion designer once called me. He had just bought a house near Compiègne.

'Paco, I know that you are interested in the supernatural. Well, I have a big problem at the moment. My friend and I cannot sleep in that house. Every night, we wake up bathed in sweat and yet frozen to the bone, having had nightmares.'

Understanding what it was all about, I asked him to invite me for the weekend. The night of my arrival, when my hosts had retired to their bedroom on the first floor, I lay down on the living room sofa and put out the light. Suddenly, in the night, I heard a violent thumping on the wall. I put on the light, the knocking stopped immediately. I went round the house to make sure that the doors and windows were closed properly. There was nobody outside. The garden was empty. I turned out the light again. The thumping immediately started again. I imagined that my friends on the first floor must be grappling with their usual nightmares. I decided to leave the light on, and there were no more noisy disturbances.

The following day I took a walk in the surrounding area. I met an old man who was working in the neighbouring garden. I told him about the events of the previous night. Suddenly, a question came into my mind: 'Tell me, what happened in that house during the First World War?'

He looked at me, astonished. 'Ah, so you know?'

'No, just an intuition. I feel a vibration. Have you any idea why the dates 1914 to 1918 come to my mind?'

He replied: 'Well, in fact . . . you see, your friend's house has the largest cellar in the village. In 1914, we were only 50 metres from the German lines and all the wounded French soldiers were put in that cellar. It was like a sick-ward. In fact, that's where they died.'

With that information, I returned to the house and asked my hosts for four candles. I placed them in the cellar and performed a little ritual. Then I went to see the village priest and asked him to hold a mass in honour of the dead. He understood the situation very well and accepted.

Since then my friends sleep very well. There are no more ghosts or nightmares. I had freed those souls who had hung on to those stones, refusing their cruel destiny and who were unable to free themselves to go towards the light, who could not reincarnate and were held prisoners between the third and fourth energy levels.

The ones who are to be pitied most are, certainly, the atheists. Convinced that their spirit is nothing but an emanation of matter and that it will not survive the decomposition of the flesh, they condemn themselves to remain in limbo, in a void! They don't believe in life after death: they will not know it! Their soul finds itself in an intermediary level, between the third and fourth energy level, in a very neutral world, very grey, uniform, like a skyless, bleak field. It is in this place that all the souls who do not believe in God end up. But I would willingly bet that one can find there those well-behaved Catholics, who refused to give credence to reincarnation, preferring to believe in that aberration which is the general resurrection of the flesh at the time of the Last Judgement. They are there, lined up, till the end of time, meaning until the big bang effaces our space-time reality; when God brings back to his bosom the immensity of the cosmos. Those souls will lie there dejected for thousands of years in a faint lethargic state, while others reincarnate, purify themselves and progress in divine joy. The seed which has not fallen on fertile ground will not elevate itself and will not come to fruition.

Obviously this is, once again, just my own personal vision. The result of my memories, of my astral voyages, my readings and reflections. The docile adepts of such and such a religion have the right to 'believe' something else. I respect their belief, just as I respect all religions. Do they not all seek to draw nearer to God, to merge with Him? Except that religions have been created by men who have tried to represent God through their personal sensitivity. I do exactly the same, you will object. The difference is a subtle one, for I do not propose a new religion. It is a fact that beliefs, dogmas and rituals are inherent to the human condition. This seems to me to allow some interpretations, without these being, necessarily, judged sacrilegious.

Furthermore, what one must not forget is that each religion transmits two kinds of knowledge. One which is readily understood, full of anecdotes and in which the expression changes from one cult to another, but the structure is similar and the objective the same: to make the elementary teachings of that particular religion available to a great number of people. The other knowledge is deeper, more esoteric. It does not contradict with the first – it complements it – but it should not be made available to everyone. It refers to the three orders, mineral, vegetable and animal and it manipulates cosmic energies. As it carries potential dangers if used for the wrong ends, it cannot be revealed lightly. It is protected by mystery and reserved for initiates.

It was to preserve that mystery that sages of all times and of every creed have disseminated their teachings under the guise of symbols, of fairy tales, of parables, legends and enigmas transmitted orally from generation to generation or in cryptic books. For the fairy tales are not just adventure stories: they can often be read on an esoteric level. 'Ali Baba and the Forty Thieves' is a good example. Ali Baba is the one who wanted to find knowledge. He was the keeper of the *sesame* which opened the doors of the cave: in fact, he descended into himself, to find that treasure, that central sun, that sacred stone. The treasure belonged to the 40 thieves – the number 40 symbolizing waiting and trial: Jesus underwent temptation in the desert for 40 days, Moses stayed 40 days at the top of Mount Sinai, Buddha and the Prophet started preaching at the age of 40. One can detect a similar meaning in 'Snow White and the Seven Dwarfs'. Snow White, the pure virgin by contrast with the pernicious step-mother, is saved by the seven dwarfs, seven as in the seven levels of matter, the seven chakras or the seven energy levels.

The same is true for the Scriptures, for if secrecy exists for the protection of a certain knowledge, it also means that each one must make the effort to follow the path of the Scriptures, by trying to understand their message. For truth cannot be conveyed like a heritage of so many gold pieces, which can be counted, evaluated and named. To name the truth would be, in fact, to reduce it. It contains a secret which can only be expressed by symbols. Dissimulation is, in this case, only a way of gaining access to the unpronounceable. Did not Jesus say: 'Let him who is able, understand!'

There are three possible levels, three ways of reading the Bible. The first is as a beautiful story, whose contradictions are, nevertheless, keys for the intuitive reader. The second is completely symbolic (Jacob's ladder is an example which everyone understands) and the third opens a door onto operational 'magic' permitting us to find God in ourselves. Equally the *Cabbala* looks for hidden secrets in the *Torah*. Certain *Cabbalists* state that the sacred text is a coded language, that the Hebraic letters correspond to numbers, each number having its own meaning, message and mystery.

Jesus often used parables to convey his message. When he said: 'No one will enter my father's kingdom lest he goes through water', he did not mean a dive, he meant prayer, meditation. Water is a symbol of prayer, of a certain form of meditation: deep meditation beyond pure and simple analysis, as the fishermen's parable seems to indicate. They threw their fishing nets to the left and caught no fish. Christ said to them: 'Throw your nets to the right' and they brought back fish. Can one imagine for one second that that story tells us Christ knew good fishing spots? Certainly not. Whereas if we look a little further, one can say that the left side of the brain is the one we use to grasp physical reality, it represents our analytic faculties. On the other hand, the right brain is the seat of abstraction and divine knowledge. When the right brain functions, there is a juncture of the two hemispheres and the opening of the third eye, the *ājna*, occurs and we perceive truth.

Later, the Gnostics and the alchemists also had to use a language which was deliberately obscure. Nostradamus hid his prophecies with puns and homophony. It was not only a question of protecting their knowledge, but also of protecting themselves from a dictatorial Church which would have burned them at the first suspicion of heresy! A book like this one, had it been written two centuries ago, would have sent me directly to the flames. An amazing fact, for not only am I in no way blaspheming, but I do not feel that I am in contradiction with the intrinsic substance of any religion. The different structures of the various cults, which engender such deadly fights nowadays, remind me of an ancient machine used in the past by cloth manufacturers, used to mangle fabrics and obtain clouded effects. To embellish and vary the appearance of the fabrics, the clothiers crushed the fabric between the cylinders of that machine, obtaining, according to the techniques used, variegated colours, undulated weaves and brushing effects, in other words, different fabrics: but the cloth remained the same.

Like these cloth manufacturers, men have invested their belief with undulating glosses, more or less luminous parables, bedecked it with myths and rituals. But the Truth remains unique in all its aspects. The saying goes that all roads lead to Rome. I prefer to think, in a more universal and egalitarian fashion, that all religions lead to God.

6

The Tearing and the Re-creation

Then I saw a new heaven, a new land
ST JOHN'S APOCALYPSE

One need not be a seer to announce the return of the spiritual in today's world: it is obvious, wherever we turn the signs are there, carried by a gigantic wave which could well become a tidal eruption. One almost forgets the formidable evolution which is taking place. Between Nietzsche's 'God is dead' and Malraux's famous 'the 21st century will be religious or it will be obliterated' what a lot of ground has been covered!

Not such a long time ago, science insisted in denying everything it did not understand. Religion was then relegated to a social activity, a soft drug or collective hysteria. Between work, family, fatherland, and the daily grind of travel-work-sleep, spirituality did not find any place in our lives.

Today some men of science seem willing to include God in their explanations of the origins of the world! Everywhere one can witness a reawakening of interest in the spiritual and supra-sensitive realms. More and more people are joining those who are on the quest towards the light. This evolution corresponds, undeniably, to a growing anguish regarding the difficult conditions experienced in daily life and the perils which threaten the future of the planet. Environmental chaos prompts us to look for a deeper meaning for our life, the attraction to the 'other side of things' then becomes a real need. For that generalized unease is matched with a sense of urgency. We feel, more and more, that our time is numbered. History has gathered speed and is dragging us down a slope which may be fatal. It is, therefore, urgent to put our life in order, so as not to be surprised by upheavals which may come about in the near future.

According to the Gnostic tradition, the first being created by God, even before the archangels, the angels or other cherubs, was Lilith, the scarlet woman. Too intelligent, too independent, she seduced some of the angels and provoked their fall. To rebalance things, God created in her image, Adam Kadmon, the scarlet man, a non-incarnated entity.

Jealous, Lilith transformed herself into a serpent to corrupt Adam: 'Look at you', said Lilith, 'You also exist, you too are God, for God created you in his image. You too, possess creative power.'

Giving in to the appeals made by this tempting voice, Adam turned away from the divine face to contemplate himself: the first egocentric gesture, which humanity would pay for dearly. Too busy looking at his belly button, Adam could no longer adore the creative energy. He was expelled from paradise and thrown into matter. He who was spirit became body. He who was androgynous was divided into two, man and woman.

Little by little incarnated man discovered his power and decided to try it out on matter. The world was there for him, he would become its master and would possess it. But to have a free hand, we had to ignore nature's sacredness. We made a simple scientific object of it, we forgot the 'why' of things to think only of the 'how'. There were no limits to our exploitation of the planet's riches. Absorbed by his Promethean activities, man became more and more estranged from God: he thus laid himself open to the most terrible retribution.

For two centuries now, 'progress' has been the catchword for humanity. Imagine! What a glorious perspective! We were going to put an end to poverty by creating abundance! Can one conceive of a simpler and a more stimulating programme? Where did it lead us, this utopian project? Our earth, our Alma Mater is today completely disfigured, eaten away like a leper's skin. The planet Earth has been in existence for millions of years. In one century – in the snapping of two fingers – we have almost exhausted the natural resources which were so generously given to us. Just one example: it is estimated that one quarter of the world's reserves of fuel have gone up in smoke. Gone up in smoke – that says exactly what it means: a very rich material, with so many uses, we are content to burn in our cars, in our houses and our factories. What spoilt children!

The same goes for trees and we would do well to dwell on this fact. The Amazon forest, a vast reservoir of living species, has lost 10 per cent of its surface, and if the devastation continues at the present rate, that forest will have disappeared within the next 70 years, in an atmosphere of generalized indifference. Africa has also been touched. In 1950, the Ivory Coast had 15 million hectares: it has no more than 3 million today. In Ethiopia, the forest represented 40 per cent of the territory in 1900; that has dwindled to about 4 per cent. Amazingly, the economic and social problems of these countries are presented as if they are nothing to do with these catastrophic environmental disasters! Deforestation has obvious consequences for the ecosystem. A great percentage of rain is generated by evaporation from the forests' trees. Furthermore, trees stabilize the soil. Consequently, if there are no more trees, there is a danger of the soil becoming arid. In Haiti, where the forest has almost completely disappeared, erosion carries away millions of cubic metres of arable land each year. Seen from the air, this country offers the sad spectacle of a poor, scruffy, despoiled land.

Why stop at that? In his blindness, man has damaged the elements which are the most vital to his survival – water and air. The rivers are completely poisoned and dying due to the foul stream of waters discharged by factories and large cities. Fish die by tens of thousands or are no longer fit for consumption. Pollution is not limited to water surfaces: certain ground waters are equally affected, others have seen their level diminish dramatically, depleted by irrigation or by excessive urban consumption. The damage runs deep. It seem that only now do we realize that water is a precious commodity. In the great capitals, the problem of water supply has started to become an issue. Water is becoming rare and one day we might have to pay a high price for a glass of drinking-water, although water is a gift from heaven.

As for the sea, we have transformed it into a dustbin, all the more so because we were convinced that it was the great purifier, capable of self-regeneration. We are beginning to perceive our error, but the damage is already considerable: we have already dumped into it all the industrial refuse, motor oil and even our radioactive waste which governments try to present as harmless!

The disorderly activities carried out by human beings also endanger the stratosphere. For a few years now we have known that the ozone layer has holes in it. That fine stratospheric layer which protects us from the sun's violent rays is damaged by the infamous chlorofluorocarbons. Already a large hole is visible over the Antarctic. And a quarter of the ozone could disappear by the year 2025! We are aware of the consequences: the ultraviolet rays may then damage our skin, our retinas, our immune systems. This menace has finally engendered a reaction – although a tardy one – on the part of governments. There is proof that the situation is becoming really dramatic. Simultaneously, the gases which produce the 'greenhouse' effect have provoked a heating of the planet which could engender droughts in various parts of the globe and a rise of the sea level, putting all the large highly populated deltas at risk.

All the dangers which pollution brings are amplified by a phenomenon which, due to its multiple consequences, certainly represents today's number one danger: I am referring to overpopulation. There are some eloquent numbers: the world population was 700 million in 1750, 1.1 billion in 1850 and 2.5 billion in 1950. In 1987 we already numbered more than 5 billion. A doubling of numbers in 37 years! Since that date another 400 million have been born, the equivalent of the whole of North America's population! By the year 2,050 the population of the planet will reach the astronomical figure of 10 billion people! And we would like to believe that the aggressions against the biosphere will not increase proportionally. How can food production possibly keep up with such a progression curve? Will we be able to solve the problem through deforestation and by the intensive use of chemical fertilizers which are so damaging to the soil?

If this rate of population growth continues, Africa will see its population multiplied tenfold in one century – 220 million in 1950 against 2 billion foreseen for the year 2050. Certain statisticians refer to that number for the year 2012! Submitted to very harsh meteorological conditions, with soils which are difficult to cultivate, will the black continent be able to face that phenomenal population explosion? Already, in the bush, women are forced to walk miles to find the water or wood necessary for survival. Desertification is gaining ground, the continent is threatened by a gigantic famine.

All the while, under the illusion of relative prosperity, the 'rich' countries feel that they are immune to those calamities. Ironically, they are the ones which have the most to lose. For it is obvious that the tens of millions of poverty stricken people will come looking for food where there is some. We must realize that the population of immigrants which causes such worry is but the beginning of a massive and inevitable 'invasion'. We are heading straight towards very pessimistic scenarios: the rich towns will erect fortifications to keep out the hungry hordes from the third world. How naïve to think that one can stop immigration with police controls! How can we imagine that a problem of planetary dimensions could find such a stupidly selfish solution?

Astonishingly, the scientific world is only now discovering what the esoterics have always known: that the planet Earth is a whole, that the elements which compose it are not compartments on which one can act without the risk of modifying its entire structure and balance. Microcosm, macrocosm – everything is in everything. To devastate the forests means altering climatic conditions; to destroy nature is to drive humanity to its ruin. Maltreated in this way, Gaia will end up by rejecting the yoke man has put on her and fight back. We have signs of that already. Not a day goes by without a natural catastrophe happening in some part of the globe. As I said at the beginning of this book, our planet is crying for help and if we continue to pretend not to hear, its future – and ours – will be threatened.

The earth's grief is all the more poignant because it has begun a period of mutation which should take it to a higher energy level. For the law of cosmic evolution dictates that everything that lives evolves onto a higher evolutionary level. Already we can perceive the signs of that mutation. When one walks on the embankment of the Seine, one notices that the trees have begun their adaptation to the fourth energy level: they are becoming silvery. That dark bottle-green which the leaves had about 50 years ago is mutating, it is becoming the colour of silver, more luminous.

Everything is mutating, the mineral realm as well as the vegetable and the animal realms. In the mines, geologists see crystals coming out of the soil. Matter is animated. Trees are changing colour. Every morning, the birds sing and sing joyously, because they too feel that universal impulse.

The only one who seems oblivious to all this, the only one who refuses to see all the evidence is man. And yet, he too is called to pass from the third to the fourth energy level, the level of the master, where *Homo sapiens* will become *Homo spiritualis*, going from rational knowledge to spirituality. Those among us who are most aware feel a revealing pain in the fontanels where the last of the chakras is, the lotus of the thousand petals which puts us in touch with the cosmic forces and wants to open to divine energy. But are the more unconscious among us going to hold back the evolution of the whole planet, in their folly of waste and destruction?

The warnings of Gaia could well become open threats, threats which can very well become reality. According to esoteric tradition, Gaia is served by the four genies: the Gnomes, red elfs which move very quickly under the ground and can sometimes be seen once night has fallen; the Sylphs who are aerial creatures; supernatural beings resembling long grey clouds which take the shape of diaphanous birds. The other elements are also inhabited, fire by the Salamanders and water by the Undines.

The earth can unleash those genies on us, as a reaction against the outrageous treatment she has suffered at the hands of man. The Gnomes have provoked earthquakes, ever more frequent, ever more lethal in the last years as we have seen in Mexico and Armenia. The Undines launch terrible floods or those terrifying tidal waves, such as Bangladesh and Eastern Asia have experienced. Salamanders light gigantic forest fires. Tens of millions of hectares have gone up in smoke in the United States and in Canada. These fires are not always the work of pyromaniacs, they are auto-cremations, reprimands addressed to men. Woe to the time when the Sylphs decide not to carry aeroplanes any longer, so making them crash. Woe to the time when the Sylphs no longer filter the ultraviolet rays of the sun!

Because we did not respect Gaia, we incur her wrath today. She will end up by seeking revenge. As we have said previously, since we behave in a negative way, she will acquire a karma which we will have imposed on her and one that only we will be able to lighten, collectively, by suffering new trials. For the law of compensation does not function on the personal level only. The faults we must atone for are not just our own sins, but also those of the group to which we belong: the crimes committed by our nation or by humanity as a whole. Thus, Germany accumulated a very heavy karma during the Second World War, a karma which it had to atone for by being cut in two for 30 years.

Faced with such a bleak world situation as the one we have today, it would be too easy exclusively to blame inconsequential governments or a capitalist society greedy for profit. Each one of us shares the responsibility. That responsibility is all the greater because the pollution is not just industrial, it is also spiritual. With our gestures and our thoughts we burden the fate of the planet with negativity.

One morning, I was walking back to my apartment in Vincennes when, suddenly, in the middle of the street, I was surrounded by darkness! My eyes, though open, could not see anything, drowned in a complete and almost palpable opacity. When that shroud brushed my skin, I cried out in terror, for that darkness had something devilish about it. That blindness only lasted one fraction of a second, but it terrified me. I hurried towards my apartment and in the meditation that followed, some images came to me. (For I don't hear voices, the messages from the beyond – 'the other side' – come to me as images.) I saw a mass of men ruminating their hatred and resentment. From their forehead oozed a black and hideous liquid which fell and coagulated on the ground. Those negative thoughts, full of hate, murder and greed were piling up and forming a viscous layer, surrounding the planet, asphyxiating it slowly.

That experience seemed to me to be a warning, like a sample of what those famous 'three nights and three days of obscurity' could be like when they descend on the world at the end of time and which the Marian prophecies speak about. For three days and three nights the sun will no longer shine, before a new sky sets in.

Confusion has taken over our activities and invaded people's spirits. People fail to think rationally and the concept of moral standards has fallen into disuse. We have never been so morally bankrupt. Who and what can we trust? What models can we adopt? There are no longer points of references. It is as if we were walking on quicksand. It is not so much the fall of Communism which astonishes us – was it not expected? It is the failure of the *status quo* which has reigned since the Second World War. The cold war at least offered us, paradoxically, a frozen view of the world which gave us relative stability. But those concepts which were our guidelines in the past are no longer viable today.

It is no use mourning the death of Communism: it led to man being treated with contempt, becoming a pawn in the manoeuvres of a totalitarian regime. That false religion, without a God, without an ideal, was nothing but the glorification of the machine, of the tractor on the field of corn. How could man have sustained that aberrant thought, to build a civilization founded on the negation of man's spiritual dimension?

But the failure of Communism does not mean the triumph of capitalism, as some people would like us to believe. Market economy, having reached a savage state, is often a wild jungle, insufficiently policed. One can see its failures in the United States: poverty, social selfishness, drugs and violence. It is a religion which worships the golden calf, in which man is crushed by the weight of gigantic companies. The only aim is material success, the will to dominate. It is no use looking in that direction to satisfy our spiritual needs. Under these conditions, one wonders which direction to take. Should we open ourselves to a universal conscience? We are much too afraid to do that! We prefer to shrink inside our shells: contraction and not dilation. We become rigid, harden ourselves by adhering to religious doctrines or nationalisms which have the advantage of providing us with a solid structural guideline.

This is what is happening with Muslim fundamentalism. The North-African and Middle-Eastern countries are confronted with difficult economic and social situations which encourage them to look for essential hope elsewhere. How can we, Westerners, feign surprise when we have a great share of responsibility for that forceful return to fundamentalism. In fact, we colonized those countries; we despised a culture which is immensely rich; we humiliated those people who were rightly proud of a great historical past; we imposed on them a way of life and an economic system; we pillaged their human and natural resources. Is it surprising that they have sought in fundamentalism a way of counteracting such humiliation, wanting to reiterate their difference? They wave the flag of fundamentalism today and apply Muslim law to the letter, forgetting its spirit.

Muslim fundamentalists have started a movement which is all the more worrying because it is only just the beginning. The Gulf War did not improve things. All the prophecies, be they Christian or Muslim, predict the renewal of the Arab flame and of their spirit of conquest. The fundamentalists see themselves as invested with a divine task, consisting of propagating their religion: by force if necessary. We are now witnessing an awakening of the Arab masses who have been crushed, be it in Algeria or on the outskirts of our towns. We are living in times which are heavy with forebodings, so threatening that we might be tempted to oppose it with another type of fundamentalism.

Parallel to these movements, and sometimes coinciding with these religious tensions, we see the development of passionate nationalisms and terrible ethnic clashes: in the Baltic countries, the Caucasus, the Balkans but also in American society. Everywhere these nationalistic movements ferment in a worrying return to a sectarian, xenophobic attitude, to a spirit of caste. Ethnic claims lead to territorial feuds and armed confrontations. At the moment when we should be achieving unity on the planet, we are caught up in fierce separatisms. Faced with growing insecurity, we close up the shutters and refuse to see what is going on outside. We have built a new tower of Babel and this resurgence seems to be emblematic of the end of this millennium. What if behind the apparent multiplicity and diversity of this fragmented world, lay one unique figure? Is there not an implacable logic in the way things are developing at present?

I had this forewarning when I went to the United States in 1965. I was invited to participate in the Ed Sullivan show, at the time the top show on CBS Television. While walking on Broadway, I was suddenly petrified to see, on the facade of a sky-scraper, in giant characters written out in luminous blue, the number 666. The words in St John's Apocalypse came back to me: (Revelation 13: 18) 'He that hath understanding, let him count the number of the beast; for it is the number of man: and his number is six hundred and sixty-six.' The beast of the apocalypse comes out of the abyss to 'direct his campaign against the saints' and to 'reign over all races, peoples, languages or nations'. Disconcerted, I asked my guide what the inscription '666' meant.

'You really don't know?' he said, astonished. 'It is the short-wave frequency of the first radio broadcast in the world.'

I was dumbfounded. There was the explanation, or rather one of the the numerous explanations for the key number 666. The beast which comes out of the abyss, could it be that radio from across the Atlantic which weaves its spider's web everywhere, while taking to the four corners of the world the songs of those 'idols' whose empty messages provoke hysteria. The young today march under the influence of their pop singers, incapable of finding a moment of silence and contemplation. It has become impossible for them to connect with God through meditation. They crowd together to hear those deafening concerts where false idols mesmerize them with red and green lights, diabolic colours.

Electric waves would be the means of propagation of the beast: by radio frequencies and also television. Does St John not warn us (Revelation 13: 11–15)?

> And I saw another beast coming out of the earth . . . and he exerciseth all the authority of the first beast in sight. And he maketh the earth and them that dwell therein to worship the first beast . . . And he doth great signs, that he should even make fire to come down out of heaven upon the earth in the sight of men. And he deceiveth them that dwell on the earth by reason of the signs which it was given him to do in the sight of the beast; saying to them who dwell on the earth, that they should make an image of the beast . . . And it was given unto him to give breath to it, even to the image of the beast, that the image should speak and cause that as many as should not worship the image of the beast should be killed.

'Animating the image of the beast', makes one immediately think of television, in front of which people remain prostrated for many hours a day, hypnotized by the fascination of that moving image which propagates its violent soap operas throughout the world, its 'variety' shows of a worrying monotony and its stupefying games. With the uncontested reign of publicity, it is now useless to influence spectators by resorting to subliminal images which are subreptiously inserted in a programme, not perceptible to the eye, but which are registered by the brain. But the danger remains and who knows to what ends this process might be used?

When we should be striving to go beyond appearances, we have even created a supplementary veil to Isis' many veils, adding another barrier to separate us from reality, by confounding fiction and fact. It is a reign of illusion for is not the great 'philosophy' of television, above all, to entertain? It is an entertainment which stops one 'thinking about oneself'.

The power of the beast is being established everywhere thanks to satellites which pick up and redistribute messages and television and radio covering the planet with a vast communications' network, which nobody can escape. Television has become a great manipulator of consciences – but has it ever been anything else? It is the most extraordinary instrument for propaganda. The Gulf War, with the control and all the tricks performed on the media, has proved that.

Apart from that, television is without a doubt the most efficient surveillance mechanism. In the underground, at work and in the street, we are increasingly being watched by cameras. We hear frequently of tele-surveillance, tele-conference, video-transmission and tele-consultation of databases. As the writer Georges Bernanos said, we can no longer speak of 'civilizations' but of 'systems'. For these communication networks, these databases, are installing a world which seems to indicate a dangerous situation: culture is disappearing to give way to hyper-planning. Backed by the research companies, television knows how to decipher our tastes and our needs, or can create them in us, tempting spectators with the delight of material consumption. It has been calculated, for example, that a child receives some 4,000 advertising messages per year!

Scenarios which were considered in the past to belong to the realm of science-fiction are becoming reality. The monopoly of communication channels leads to an aseptic totalitarianism. Man becomes a simple pawn in a mechanical system. The development of computers has reduced us all to numbers. Our identity in life has become a magnetized card which allows us to eat, buy petrol or an air ticket and so on.

All this information is assembled and studied by databases which can know, in this way, how we live, how much we earn and what we do with our money.

Under the pretext of reinforcing security, a system is being tested whereby electronic identity cards would actually be studied and linked to a central computer. They would provide all sorts of information on individual persons. Some even dream of inserting electronic devices under the skin. Let us take another look at St John's Apocalypse (Revelation 13: 16–17):

> And he causeth all, the small and the great, and the rich and the poor, and the free and the bond, that there be given them a mark on their right hand or upon their forehead and that no man should be able to buy or sell, save that he hath the mark, even the name of the beast or the number of his name.

Do not mistake my intentions. I do not want to pass for a reactionary preacher. Far be it from me to question the benefits of a technology whose inventions I have greeted in my way, in my collections. Science and its prodigies have brought us a knowledge, a freedom of movement which our ancestors did not enjoy. But that is no reason for not paying attention to the finalities of this so-called progress. It is the negative use of these inventions which is dangerous. The beast is all the more dangerous because it is very seductive.

Has the apocalypse started? Judging from all the worrying signs which we have just mentioned, we are justified in asking the question. But, before going any further in the evocation of the disturbances to come, we must remind the reader that 'apocalypse' does not mean 'total destruction of the world', it actually means 'revelation'. Revelation of the origins and revelation of divine light. But that revelation will not come about smoothly and all will not be saved. Terrible things will happen and are already happening.

The sorcerer's apprentice who wanted to try out his divine

powers ended up by creating an atomic arsenal which can destroy the whole planet, by mechanical destruction or by pollution. In St John's book, the Revelation to John, after the opening of the seventh seal, the seven angels sound the trumpet to announce the imminence of the Last Judgement. When the third angel rings, it is said (Revelation 8: 10–11):

> And there fell from heaven a great star, burning a torch, and it fell upon the third part of the rivers and upon the fountain of the waters; and the name of the star is called Wormwood: and the third part of the waters became wormwood; and many men died of the waters because they were made bitter.
>
> (*) Wormwood (*Artemisia absinthium*) is a plant with a bitter, slightly aromatic taste, now chiefly used in making absinthe.

One immediately thinks that waters 'made bitter' could be due to major technological risks such as pollution of chemical or radioactive origin. But very few people know that the wormwood mentioned by St John translates in Ukranian to a name which has echoed around the world like gunpowder! Chernobyl, that Soviet nuclear station which caused the greatest nuclear disaster of all time, with the result that contamination spread millions of kilometres around. The most incredulous will at least see a troubling coincidence.

The fourth trumpet, has it already rung? (Revelation 8: 12)

> And the fourth angel sounded, and the third part of the sun was smitten, and the third part of the moon and the third part of the stars, that the third part of them should be darkened and the day should not shine for the third part of it . . .

Today the sun's spots are visible to the naked eye. The great Michael of Notre-Dame, alias Nostradamus, had also brought the 'sun's defects' to our attention:

> When the default of the sun will come about
> In daylight the monster will be seen

> Will be interpreted otherwise
> The price to be paid nobody will have predicted

'Will be interpreted otherwise' rings true, for we must admit that all the signs and the warnings are consciously denied. We prefer to cover our eyes. On all levels we decidedly practise the ostrich's strategy. Politicians look at ecology as a simple gadget to be used during elections and industrialists see it as a stumbling-block. Nations are plunged in non-ending procrastination. As for the man in the street, he feels confusedly that he is in danger, but is comforted by the media and tells himself that if there are going to be environmental calamities, they will probably take place after his death anyway.

St John tell us (Revelation 9: 1):

> And the fifth angel sounded, and I saw a star from heaven fallen unto the earth; and there was given to him the key of the pit of the abyss. And he opened the pit of the abyss; and there went up a smoke out of the pit, as the smoke of a great furnace; and the sun and the air were darkened by reason of the smoke of the pit.

The smoke of the oil wells in Kuwait, did they not invade the sky to mingle with the fumes of Japanese volcanoes or those of the Philippines? And added to those physical fumes are spiritual fumes, born of the chaos which reigns among spirits, of false values and of that human negativity which drives many people to the abyss.

As for the last trumpet sounding, John tells us this (Revelation 11: 18):

> And the nations were wrath, and thy wrath came, and the time of the dead to be judged, and the time to give their reward to thy servants the prophets, and to the saints, and to them that fear thy name, the small and the great; and to destroy *them* that destroy the earth.

145

The Earth is not the first planet to incur divine wrath. It is said in Gnosis and in the revelations of the masters that there existed, between Earth and Jupiter, 5 million years ago, a planet called Traïa. That planet too had reached a stage where it was going to pass on to another energy level, but could not do so due to the sacrileges committed by the humanoids who inhabited it. It exploded, provoking a rain of asteroids which bombarded the solar system, and the impact can be seen on Mercury, Mars, the moon and the Earth. Will the Earth meet the same fate as Traïa?

Astronomers have recently identified a meteorite baptized '1990 Mu', whose path is not yet known for sure, but which could make the moon disintegrate, destroy the Earth or pass sufficiently close to destroy the atmosphere and transform our planet into a ball of fire. Fantastic theory? Statistically the probability is small, but it is nonetheless real. Recent scientific theory states that the end of the reign of the dinosaurs could have been provoked by a meteorite which, by brushing against the Earth, had set the forests on fire and burned those giant animals. One finds, in fact, in secondary sediments a fine black pellicule which contains microscopic diamonds issued from a meteorite. Vestige of the greatest furnace of all time? Prefiguration of a coming cataclysm? The Apocalypse speaks of a dragon of fire whose tail sweeps a third of the stars from the sky and throws them to Earth (12: 4). No doubt determined by divine will, the end of the dinosaurs allowed for the appearance of man, who was able to reign over all things. But he has made bad use of the supremacy which was given to him, over nature and other living creatures. Is the end of *Homo sapiens* approaching?

I would not dare to mention dates. This would be far too risky. Let us remember the prophecy of St Malachias establishing the list of 111 popes who, since Celestine II, would be in office before the Last Judgement. If we believe Malachias, the

Antichrist, the false prophet personifying the beast, will come on earth after the death of Pope Peter II, called the Roman. And John-Paul II will be the one before last. Saint Clement has also warned us: woe to the times when the name of the Pope will start with a K! Well, John-Paul II's Polish first name is Karol!

The present Pope has in his possession the three secrets delivered by the Virgin to the three shepherds at Fatima in 1917. One knows that the first two were visions of the hell that was the Second World War. What is the third? Why does John-Paul II refuse to reveal it? Is it so dreadful? Yet, the Pope received a warning from heaven when there was an attempt to assassinate him on the anniversary of the revelation of the Virgin's messages at Fatima. Are we going to have to wait for Nostradamus' prophecy in Century 2, quatrain 97, to come to pass?

> Roman pontiff do not approach
> The city which two rivers bathe
> Your blood will nearby be spilt
> You and yours when the rose will bloom

Or in Century 18, quatrain 46:

> 'Pol Mensolé' [Paul – the travail of the sun] will die near the river Rhône, having fled near the passes of Tarascon [and Beaucaire], for Mars [war] will do terrible things to the throne [of St Peter], then in France there will be three allies, the King of France [the rooster] and the United States [the eagle].

Pol Mensolé, according to some, is the Polish pope. According to these prophecies he will meet his death near the Rhone, in a town bathed by two rivers. Note the strange last phrase evoking the 'three point brothers'. Set out in a triangle, the three points form an esoteric symbol used by Masons. Is a violent Masonic lodge going to plan a killing which would mark the announced fall of the Pauline Church, the great courtesan of the apocalypse?

Without fixing the year or the day, the truth is that time is running short. There is a generalized feeling of urgency. Everything goes very fast now. Each week we verify an acceleration of these weighty menaces which all seem to be on the increase, overpopulation, pollution. It is as if humanity was on board a train going at great speed towards a huge buffer-stop. And even the most discerning drivers are content only to mumble that we must go slower. We see developing before our eyes a feverish culture. As if people sense that time is 'short', man is in love with speed whatever its form. Everything has to be 'instantaneous', this is the age of the fax machine and other instruments designed to speed our activities.

This urgency, one finds equally in the application of karmic law. Whereas before, if one committed a fault, retribution would come in another life, now everything is accelerated. If we make a bad choice, be it in our professional life or in our emotional or spiritual life, the sanction is almost immediate. I see this tendency all around me. The slightest slip is paid for at once. We must, therefore, be doubly vigilant. It is as if we were going to condense several existences into one. But rather than be afraid, we must see this as an extraordinary opportunity for quick progress. We must try and be in harmony with ourselves and others. Why continue to put off good actions till tomorrow? Let us act in the present, let us lighten our karma while there is still time!

The most cynical among us may ask themselves why make such an effort if the Earth must disappear? Why, on the contrary, can we not give free rein to all our vile instincts? Why not rob a bank and live the rest of our days in opulence and leisure? That is to forget an essential fact: humanity's crazy race towards destruction is not irreversible! If man finally becomes conscious of the situation's gravity, the planet can still be saved.

This is how one should interpret the numerous apparitions of the Virgin Mary which have punctuated the last century. The Virgin, who is all compassion, takes pity on man and wants to warn him, remind him of his duties. Wherever she has chosen to appear, the Virgin's message has been the same, be it Rue du Bac in Paris, at La Salette near Grenoble, Fatima in Portugal, Dozulé near Lisieux: 'I love you and I do not want your condemnation. Pray! Ask for forgiveness! Elevate yourselves! Turn towards Christ, or otherwise . . .'

By praying we can gather together pure energies which will combat the general darkness. Thus, in monasteries and other prayer centres, men and women try and reject the darkness by creating 'bubbles' of hope. Furthermore, there are exceptional beings, known as 'avatars', who accept reincarnation to try and absorb the masses of negativity which envelop the earth. In India, there is an extraordinary being, an avatar, named Saï Baba who has come to stop that country from succumbing to murderous folly. Such beings of light are capable of healing people, simply by laying hands on them: they take upon themselves the karma of other human beings and thus liberate them from their faults. At least these will, perhaps, be able to escape the cataclysm.

For there will be survivors! The Bible says that those who will be spared are only those who are inscribed in the Book of the Life of the Lamb . . . 'Hurt not the earth, neither the sea, nor the trees, till we shall have sealed the servants of God on their foreheads.' (Revelation 7: 3)

Is 'sealed . . . on their foreheads' not a reference to those who have succeeded in opening the ājna, the third eye situated in the middle of the forehead, meaning those who have awoken to spirituality, who are in touch with the cosmic whole and who, consequently, will be able to have access to the new world of light. For, once more, the apocalypse is not the end of the world but only the end of *this* world.

We are at the dawn of a new age. The Kali-Yuga cycle, or

age of steel, is coming to an end. We are going to enter a new golden age, the era of Aquarius, placed under the sign of the highest spirituality, of crystal-like purity. But it is no use fooling ourselves. To have access to that celestial Jerusalem, we will have to 'clean the Augeas' stables'. The passage will be difficult, all the prophecies concur. The population will be decimated, the earth washed. Criminally blind men must finally acknowledge their misdeeds. For a new plant to grow, for a new flower to bloom, it is first necessary for the shell of the seed to soften and the seed to bury itself in the earth and germinate. The same is true for civilizations which, as we know, are mortal.

A spiritual era is announced. The unfolding of events itself proclaims it. It forecasts that man will undergo a terrible crisis. Social chaos will reign when the mega-cities are transformed into veritable jungles, where man will once again behave like a wolf towards his fellow man. Then an awakening will take place, a realization that humanity's survival requires solutions on a planetary scale. Resources will be better administered, the vital importance of education and fraternity will be understood and these will become necessary values. Only then will man have access to a third phase, one in which he will explore the depths of his soul. He will discover his oneness with the cosmos. The initiate will become the adept. Man will finally be fulfilled.

You see how wrong it would be to take me for a prophet of doom. If I have insisted heavily on the perils which await us, it is not due to a morbid taste for disaster, nor because I see myself as an avenging prophet. My 'message' is a message of hope. If there is going to be a change of cycle, it is certainly for the best and we have in our hands the means which will allow us greatly to facilitate the transition. To do this, we have to continue patiently to work on ourselves, free ourselves of any selfish, negative thoughts and cultivate positive feelings, the most generous: I am talking of love, of course – real love.

7

The Seamless Tunic

Let us love one another,
for love comes from God
THE FIRST EPISTLE OF JOHN

The future could bring cruel trials. But whatever happens, we must continue to live – and evolve – in the present. A present which the urgency of our time makes even more precious. With or without the apocalypse, our quest must continue. First of all because, as we have seen, we all have a role to play in the safeguard of our planet. Secondly, because a great objective is before us, the ascension to higher energy levels to finally reintegrate the primal oneness. Whatever the outer pressures, we should by our daily actions, purify our body and our soul to achieve serenity. After all, what do trials matter if they are the necessary stages to attain a 'revelation', that of our deeper self and of our kinship with God!

St John tells us 'God is love' in his first Gospel (John 4: 7). To be a divine reflection, we should cultivate in ourselves that extraordinary force, we should become 'love'. But do we know what that actually means? There are two words which our modern world has persisted in corrupting: 'God' and 'love'. Perhaps, because these notions are almost impossible to conceive and are, therefore, subject to all kinds of distortions. This may also be because those in power, sensing the 'revolutionary' force and the reality behind these two words, have done everything to defuse and weaken their meaning by vulgarizing them and confining them to restricting structures.

The Pauline Church itself has imposed on its members the image of an anthropomorphic God, presenting him sometimes as a kind old man, at other times as a ferociously strict father who pokes his nose into people's business, or who is called to rescue the faithful at an opportune moment like a *deus ex machina*. That's the easy way! In the same way, love has been overexposed, associated with the vulgar carnal appetite or, at best, seen as a passion which is both uncontrolled and ephemeral. As for real love, that has been relegated to the rank of historic curiosities.

Sexuality is certainly not negligible. We have seen that it can awaken in us the intuition of the primordial unity. But having been twisted and muddied, one wonders if the sexual act has not simply become, more often than not, a way of satisfying a biological need? To hope to touch the sacred, one has to go through an act of sublimation, which means giving sexuality its total dimension. Just as the sexual act, love should be sifted for impurities. Is love not corrupted by parasitical feelings? The first of which is the desire for possession. Is it not a question of attracting the other to oneself and draining him or her of their energy, of smothering them? All these are contracting, therefore negative, conceptions. There is no field with as many war-like metaphors as love. One would think that one goes courting as one starts a war campaign: one must vanquish the adversary's resistance and obtain complete surrender. Love has become conquest. Every kind of trick is allowed. To love in this way means wanting the partner to bend to our will, taking him or her prisoner.

What is all this fire for, if not to satisfy our own pride, to prove to ourselves that we can seduce? Nobody is exempt from vanity. Who would dare to deny that we seek a person's favours more for our pleasure than for theirs? The game of love, far from being the discovery of the other, is, most of the time, played to satisfy our own ego. This egotism is even apparent in our language: do we not say *my* wife, *my* husband? As if to state that they belong to us and are the object of our goodwill.

We are all a bit narcissistic. And, of course, one has to be capable of loving oneself which, as we have seen, is an essential stage. There can be no real progress until we can say: 'I love myself' which is, in fact, very different from a narcissistic declaration. This love of oneself is the consciousness that we have been created by God, in his image. There is no question of pride here: it means accepting oneself by recognizing the divine spark which lives in us. One must love oneself because of what God has made of us and not for the image one gives the world. That is true love's primordial condition. Christ said 'love your neighbour as *you love yourself!*', for one is not possible without the other.

How can one possibly love another, if one does not love oneself? How can one trust another, if one does not trust oneself? To love another is not such a simple project as it might appear at first. In our choice of love, we are subject to multiple illusions. The attraction we feel for someone is due, for the most part, not to the real person but to the image which we have of him or her, to outer 'qualities' such as beauty, success and riches. As soon as these images fade, love disappears with them.

But on a deeper level, is that perpetual search for one's lost 'other half' not false from the start and therefore illusory? Let us recall that, at the very moment of our incarnation, our being was suddenly cut in two, painfully. That being who was androgyne on an energy level is now man or woman on earth. In other words, it is ourselves that we are looking for in another and we sometimes spend our lives searching for

153

something which is buried deep within us. We beg fate to put this love in our path, when it would 'suffice' to descend within ourselves. For our other half sleeps within us, hidden in the liver, that essential organ where our various links with the cosmos are imprinted. As long as we are not conscious of this, the quest for love will remain disappointing. You may object that there are couples who are perfectly happy. This is because they have found a compromise which comes close to their primordial oneness. But I feel that there will always be a deep yearning within us, inherent to our human condition.

It can happen that, in a relationship, one approaches the alchemy we have dreamed of. Instinctively, one feels analogies, obvious correspondences with the other. Those who have known such experiences know that, at least in the first moments, there is no desire to possess the other person, but simply a desire to merge with him or her. Unfortunately, that passionate love is often ephemeral, condemned to failure, I'm sorry to say. The scission which we undergo when we incarnate contains the origin, but also the futility of our amorous quest. As an inspired poet once wrote 'There is no happy love'. The need for fusion in itself reveals that we are still prone to an egocentric attitude which bodes no good, even if lived *a contrario*. Love is to open oneself to the other and not devour or to let oneself be absorbed.

We must also remember that the notion of the couple is not inherent to all civilizations. In Amazonia there are tribes in which men and women are divided into two 'houses'. They frequently change partners and the children are brought up together in a third 'house'. For those indians, the idea of a couple is meaningless. In the West, it has been imposed by Judeo-Christian law which saw in it, without doubt and not without common sense, a means of avoiding social anarchy and sexual license which threatened to make people stray from their faith or simply keep them from going to church. The fidelity sworn at the altar was, consequently, ratified by our own possessive instinct and perpetuated by a respect for tradition. But are all traditions to be followed? After all, some Judeo-Christian dogmas led to the Inquisition and to religious conflicts. Is Christian marriage the best way to individual fulfilment? A cynical poet wrote: 'Unable to do away with love, the Church disinfected it and created marriage.'

The glorification of procreation was certainly proclaimed with the same spirit. When the Jews arrived in Palestine, led by Moses, they numbered a few thousand. Therefore, the order was: 'Grow and multiply. Accursed be the dry fruits.' Christian civilizations have followed suit. One must have children, so as to provide labour to handle either spades or guns.

Coupledom, love in twos, is therefore at best an imitation of fundamental oneness, at worst only a habit. In both cases, it usually comes down to an appropriation of one person by the other. To really love would mean, on the contrary, to give the other everything, to go towards our love and not attract the other to oneself. It does not mean to cover the beloved with gifts, which are but disguised chains, but to give of oneself, to listen, to be available. Such a disinterested attitude is closer to divine love. But what we must understand is that that love should not be reserved for one person. The fact that we choose a soul mate in the present life, decide to procreate, opt for fidelity and a good sexual relationship does not mean that we should not love the whole of humanity. This may sound naïve to some, but it is the only way to find harmony and to avoid being a victim of hate. On every occasion, one must approach the other in a positive way. By doing this, one realizes that the outer negativity which may exist is diffused. It loses its purpose or boomerangs back to the one who emits it.

One must never give way to rage. Anger is contracting: one says 'I am on edge', 'It gets on my nerves'. Whereas everything becomes simple when one is open. Someone who is completely open, docile and available is never attacked. We say that the serpent does not bite the hermit, because the animal senses that the hermit wishes it no harm. It is a well known fact that dogs bare their teeth to people who approach them with bad intentions or with fear, whereas love knows no fear. The same applies to travelling on the underground. I firmly believe that the more we fear aggression, the more chance we have of being victimized. Having left the animal state, man has kept its instincts. Do we not immediately perceive when the person in front of us is hostile? That is just when we should avoid 'blocking'. With a little kindness, if we are malleable and receive each person with a smile, welcome them calmly, all goes well. Astonishingly, kindness is *disarming*. In fact, people will attack those who, deep down, have an undercurrent of aggression. The two negative poles clash and reject each other. When we have no hate in ourselves, nobody comes to attack us. Love is the best form of protection.

I will be thought of as a dreamer. People will object that this 'method' although very efficient is not really pertinent to daily life, for good resolutions cannot always be kept. It is all very well, but life is a battle, the world is a jungle and to go around as meek as a lamb, risking one's neck, is not always the best course of action. Professional life, to mention but one aspect, is full of dishonest or envious people whose only objective is to abuse our candour. But when we speak of applying honesty and an open mind, this does not mean being a simpleton. It is not a question of lowering one's guard, but of refusing to play the aggressor. We should never approach people with our spirit filled with prejudices and preconceived ideas, for not to attack is also not to judge. We should accept people as they come, as they are. To judge someone is to imprison that person in a mould, to impose limits on them and by doing that, we are limiting ourselves. 'Do not judge and you will not be judged . . . For the measure you use will be used on you.' (Matthew 7: 1.) Obviously, we have the right to choose our friends or to have preferences, according to affinities which are often dictated by the fact that those people are on the same wavelength, the same energy level, as ourselves. Nevertheless, we should never judge. We should also avoid lying. For to lie is to despise the other person, to show no respect for him. Lying often suits us, for it is sometimes very convenient. But, let us not forget that it makes our karma heavier.

Having said that, it is true that these elementary moral principles are easy to formulate, but not so easy to practise. A humorist remarked that it is much easier to love humanity in general than your next-door neighbour. We are tempted to judge at every moment. That man with such odd clothes in the street, that friend who has played a trick on us, that girl who trades on her looks, and so on. Nevertheless, something should make us reflect: we are all the more ready to judge others if we do not really know them, promptly criticizing them if we have no idea what moves them, no inkling of their motives! On the other hand, as soon as it is somebody we love, judgement makes way for good will: we are ready to accept and help them even if we don't understand their reasons.

The secret which allows us not to judge is humility, that queen of virtues, so simple and yet so rare. Rare because the whole of our personality opposes it; simple because reason itself has convinced us of the need to be humble. For we are all, every one of us, a parcel of the whole, a cell of the divine cosmos. Why should a drop of water despise the next drop of water? They are strictly identical, a part and a reflection of the ocean in which they find their reason for existing. When I find myself before another person, I know and I feel that in spite of superficial differences, we have the same origin, the same hope to solve the unease which is our condition on earth.

In fact we are made of the same fabric. It is perhaps to illustrate this that the Bible tells us that Christ wore a *seamless* tunic. He, therefore, embodied the universality of the human condition and the universality of his message. No seam, meaning no barrier, no frontier. The word of Christ has nothing in common with a patchwork made of different fabrics. His message is unique: 'Love your neighbour as you love yourself, for God is in you.'

The purest love we can feel is of divine inspiration. But to revive this feeling we have to silence our mental babble, to 'put out Seth's furnace' which wants to rationalize everything. Our rational mind is Satan's. He weighs our interests, attaches us to someone for our own self-interest, sometimes unconsciously. We have to go beyond that negative apprehension of the other, so as to be able to receive him as a brother, another self. If our rational mind insists on differentiation, our 'feeling' will, on the contrary, bring us together with others, emphasizing our similarities. Let us remember that Jesus Christ showed his heart and said: 'This is the entrance to the kingdom of God'. In other words the discovery of God is within the domain, not of analysis, but of intuition. 'God is sensitive to the heart' said Pascal. It is the famous formula: God cannot be proved, he can only be felt.

Of course, we must understand the heart not as the organ of the affections, but as what man has that is deepest. On the solar plexus, near the heart, there is a chakra which is the seat of our inner God, in the image of God the Father. With meditation, one can awaken this energy centre, so as to 'feel' that we are inhabited by the divine, as is all creation. God gave the creative impulse, the cosmic Virgin gave form to all things, Christ animated them with the verb. Everything on earth is alive, from minerals to man: everything moves, vibrates and develops. The world obeys the law of involution and evolution: the involution of spirit in matter and evolution towards the subtle, disincarnated body. The plant ascends from the earth towards the sun; the stone transmutes into crystal and becomes light. In the same way, man wants to reach higher energy levels, nearer the sun, that beacon of truth and justice.

This law of universal ascension is none other than the impetus towards God, towards that supreme energy which is a colossal vibrational centre around which the cosmos structures itself. That vibration which has come from primordial origins and is present in all things, can be heard in ourselves. We have to listen. It means recovering through prayer the primordial sound which puts us in harmony with the cosmos and with the whole.

But there is prayer and prayer; I started with the vocal prayer, the litanies, words strung together pronounced one after the other. One day, I surprised myself praying like that: I mumbled sentences to which I no longer paid attention. How could God have heard me? Then I meditated on each word. 'Our Father who art in Heaven . . .' Let us just try to conceive this! One can spend an hour imagining all the possibilities in the words 'Our Father', creator of all men on earth.

Today, my prayer is rarely formulated. It consists mainly of creating an inner void and of imposing total silence on myself. Once this is accomplished, I try and amplify the vibration which emanates from the heart. First of all, I see a pink golden light which dilates all the pores of the skin and all the cells of my body. The answer comes quickly: a light comes and hits me like a thunderbolt. I feel as if I am going to explode, scattering my atoms in space. How can I put such intense joy into words?

Meditation allows us to have direct access to God. We don't need an intermediary, as the Pauline Church would have us believe, having imposed all of its Episcopalian hierarchy as a screen between the faithful and God. Through love and prayer we can communicate with God. That is what Islam has understood so well: the great strength of the Koran is precisely that, it is a hymn of love from man to God, without an intermediary. Sufism, that Muslim asceticism, has particularly developed this notion of sacred love which permits us to merge with the divine during our life on earth.

God created us out of love. Everything has been conceived out of love, even the daily problems which trouble us. These are lessons and trials to incite us to think about and to correct our faults. If we become persuaded by that, our vision of the world becomes luminous. A problem has arisen? Thank heaven and try and learn a lesson for the future. Someone wishes you ill? Wish him the best! It is obviously very difficult, annoying and inconceivable for our self-esteem and our pride. But it is, nevertheless, a source of strength and extra-ordinary well-being. 'Love your enemies and pray for those who persecute you', St John tells us. Then a profound and wonderful transformation will occur in your daily life. It is the great cleansing. Body and soul will be delivered of their dross and attain inner peace. The blindfold of negativity which covered our eyes will disappear. Divine light will no longer be obstructed.

The man or woman that you were becomes transformed. It is not necessary to wait until one has reached the higher energy levels. Joy can be achieved right here. But for this to happen, one has to 'let the old man decay', meaning the material, egotistical and rational man in us, to become the younger, open man. That is a symbolic death, which one finds in all initiation rituals. As in the empty tomb at Cheops, which the neophyte penetrated, or the rites that African children undergo, buried up to their necks with just their head out of the earth, with a cloth on their face to be able to breathe. When the child is disinterred, he has died symbolically; the new man, the initiate, has just been born. The doctrine of reincarnation promises us a rebirth in another life. But we must not forget that we have come here to accomplish the renaissance of the new man, the spiritual man, the child of Aquarius.

The law of love, that basic pillar of all Christian religions, whether Jewish, Muslim or Oriental, is the counterbalance and corrector of the law of karma. Thanks to love, we have the extraordinary possibility of solving our past faults and suspending the law of cause and effect. From then on, the jewel which was hidden in the depth of our being can shed its cover and shine brightly. We have finally developed all the potential in our being. From that fulfilment a deep, profound joy is born which is not an illusion. In effect, once we have chosen this path, we receive answers and blazes of energy which put us in touch with other realms that are mineral, vegetable and animal. In other words, there is a physical result, internal, concrete, which is more than serenity: it is a foretaste of the absolute.

Relieved of his karma, the initiate can finally hope to conceive these inexpressible notions which are Eternity and Infinite, that is to say, God. Since God is totality, He must unite us in our quest, instead of separating us in the fanatical defence of personal or group convictions. Each religion represents an approach to divine light, with its share of knowledge, fragmented, no doubt, because of false interpretations, unless it be because of specious intentions. But whatever the paths we take, which sometimes mislead us, the idea of a common route should incite us to collaborate and help each other to efface our errors, instead of killing each other to impose our all-too-human certitudes.

There remain the atheists, fated to non-existence in the future, in my view. But I feel sure that there are many more agnostics or sceptics than atheists and that a so-called non-believer who seeks to do good and practises the law of love is nearer God, whatever he thinks, than an iniquitous believer.

As for me, if I have shocked the sensitivity of certain readers due to my own interpretations and my vision of the world, I beg their pardon. I had no intention of flaunting the truth, but of describing the mysteries which have led me little by little to that truth. It is a truth that is permanently refashioned, corrected by doubt and prudence, all through the existences of this eternal self, incarnated today as a certain Paco Rabanne.

Five billion individuals, presently on earth, are called to undertake the same quest. Eternity and light are the aims of this voyage. Those who are afraid of the distance which separates us from these goals should remember that, in spite of the adversity, the ultimate beauty of this journey resides not only in arriving at our destination, but also in the path travelled.

Index